REDISCOVER JOY WITH YOUR DOG

How to Train Your Dog
to Live in Harmony with Your Family

YVONNE DONE

REDISCOVER JOY WITH YOUR DOG

How to Train Your Dog
to Live in Harmony with Your Family

Yvonne Done

**AUTHOR
ACADEMY** elite

Published by Author Academy Elite

PO Box 43, Powell, OH 43065

www.AuthorAcademyElite.com

Identifiers:

Paperback: 979-8-88583-180-2

Hardback: 979-8-88583-181-9

Ebook: 979-8-88583-182-6

Library of Congress Control Number: 2023900834

Available in paperback, hardback, e-book, and audiobook

All Scripture quotations, unless otherwise indicated, are taken from the Holy Bible, New International Version®, NIV®. Copyright © 1973, 1978, 1984 by Biblica, Inc.™ Used by permission of Zondervan. All rights reserved worldwide.

Any Internet addresses (websites, blogs, etc.) and telephone numbers printed in this book are offered as a resource. They are not intended in any way to be or imply an endorsement by Author Academy Elite, nor does Author Academy Elite vouch for the content of these sites and numbers for the life of this book.

Some names and identifying details have been changed to protect the privacy of individuals.

This book is dedicated to Fred. Although you are gone, you will never be forgotten. You taught me so much about creating an authentic and happy relationship with a dog.

TABLE OF CONTENTS

FOREWORD xi

INTRODUCTION 1
    J–Join Your Dream with Reality... 8
    O–Overcoming the Roadblocks to Your Dreams 8
    Y–Yes, to Daily Games That Make a Difference. 9
    D—Dog on a Mission... 10
    O—Out and About—Training for the Situation, Not in the Situation 11
    G—Game Plans—Understanding That Dog Training Is 24/7 11

PART I: WHAT IT IS TO BE HUMAN

Chapter 1: JOIN THE DREAM WITH THE REALITY 19
    Knowing Your Powerful Why 20
    Understanding Yourself.. 22
    Give Yourself Permission 23

Chapter 2: OVERCOMING THE ROADBLOCKS 26
    A Roadblock Is a Pointer, Not a Disappointment. 29
    Failing Forward.. 30
    Hope Deferred Makes the Heart Sick 34

Chapter 3: YES, TO GAME PLANS... 38
    Me Human—You Dog.. 38
    The Science of Communication 41
    The Gift of Curiosity.. 46

PART II: WHAT IS A DOG?

Chapter 4: DOG ON A MISSION.. 62
    Dogmanship.. 64
    What Is a Dog? 65
    Dogs on a Mission and Family Therapy 69

Chapter 5: OUT AND ABOUT 76
    The Plight of a Working Dog... 79
    Using Your Dog's Opus.. 81
    Breed Needs.. 82

Chapter 6: GAME PLANS...91

   Brain Games..93

   Training versus Play...95

   Rediscover Joy with Your Dog 97

EPILOGUE 103

   The Joy of Dog Game-Plan Vision Worksheets.............................103

   Remember the Three for Three Rule..124

   Harmony House Management...124

   Food Rations and Training Treats 132

   House Training...134

   Troubleshooting 136

   What a Difference a Breed Makes...137

   Game-Plan Games to Add to Your Worksheets 142

   Collar Grab Game 142

   Distraction Game Level One 142

   Say Hellos Game 144

   Swapsies...146

   Troubleshooting 147

   Tug Training...149

   Playing Tug Games with Your Puppy or Dog................................149

   Troubleshooting 150

   Whip It Game 151

   Troubleshooting 152

   Scent Games 152

   Searching for a Person...153

   Troubleshooting 154

   Think About It Games versus 'Leave It.' 155

   Think About It Game 155

   Get It Game 156

   Greeting Games—Children/Elderly and Puppies/Dogs 158

   Troubleshooting 161

   Teaching Your Dog Recall (Coming Back to You When You Call)

  162

   Troubleshooting 164

   Loose Leash Games 164

   Follow My Hand Game..164

   Follow Me in Circles...165

   Troubleshooting 166

   Transition Games 166

Example of a Transition—Going for a Walk 167

Troubleshooting 168

This Way Game—Switching Direction. 168

Troubleshooting 170

Chase Me Game 170

Distraction Game Level Two 171

Pop Up Game—Going to Bed 172

Pop Up Game 173

Calm Game 174

Troubleshooting 174

Mouse Trap Game—Another Version of the Think About It Game

.... 174

Troubleshooting 176

ACKNOWLEDGMENTS **177**

ABOUT THE AUTHOR **179**

FOREWORD

DR SUNIL K. RAHEJA
Pursuer of Wisdom
Author of the Book, Dancing with Wisdom
Psychiatrist and Coach

I once told Yvonne when she was in full flow explaining her training techniques, "I just want to enjoy my dog." She tells me it was at that point this book was born. Yvonne's book does indeed set out to convince the everyday dog owner that they can rediscover joy with their dog, whether you have a new dog in the household or an older dog misbehaving.

This book follows the quest to understand the relationship between a dog and its owner. Indeed, Yvonne admirably explains what it is to be human, what a dog is and how the two species come together to form a partnership. However, she does not take the usual approach of setting out to show you how to train your dog. Instead, Yvonne leads the owner on a journey of self-discovery, where she encourages the readers to stay curious.

As she outlines how training a dog can impact our emotions, we are given glimpses of Yvonne's journey to what she calls 'doggy enlightenment'. On this journey, Yvonne found people focused on fixing what was wrong with her dog rather than wondering how Yvonne felt at the other end of the lead. She admitted, 'they all wanted to fix my dog, but I knew it was me that needed fixing. I knew I needed to change how I did things, but I didn't know how until I discovered how to write a new story for my dog and me.'

Yvonne outlines how the reader can also write a new story for their dog, as she found that writing herself as the hero guide in her dogs' stories gave her the traction to make the right choices. Yvonne shares how we are always training our dogs whether we realise it or not. She then explains the dog's point of view and how our emotions affect our dogs and vice versa. Happily, she does not leave the reader without solutions to the many typical dog-owning problems. There is an extremely useful Epilogue to the book outlining her approach to intentional training techniques that can be incorporated into everyday life.

Like many people, I own a pet dog that is not exceptionally well trained. However, our little white crossbreed, whom all the family dearly loves, has taught us more about ourselves than we thought possible. We have had to negotiate as a family our own set of expectations. Also, as with all families, we have all had to make adjustments and compromises. With much encouragement, Yvonne gives us hope to make minor adjustments in our daily activities to achieve the dog of our dreams. Instead of being an accidental dog trainer, Yvonne encourages every owner to be more intentional about what everyday life teaches their dog.

Yvonne and I are followers of the teachings of Jesus Christ, and like me, Yvonne believes that dogs are a gift from God that also teaches us how to be more human.

Enjoy this book and enjoy your dog!

INTRODUCTION

"Dogs do speak, but only to those who know how to listen." —Orhan Pamuk

Like many of my readers, I wondered what joy I might gain from my shoe chewing, car chasing, and poo-producing machine that was my new dog. I had reached the buffers of my patience. My new puppy, who had a working dog heritage, did not behave like any dog I had ever owned. I had lost the joy of those first puppy kisses, which gladdened the heart. However, I survived the experience and learned what a dog really is and the difference between a pet and a working dog. Furthermore, in my bid to help Fred adjust to our urban life, I became fascinated by the subject of canine ethology, the science of dog behaviour. As I sought out all I could about the topic, I realised that not only was my dog talking to me, but I had to learn how to listen.

Some thirteen years later, with my old dog Fred sitting at my feet whilst writing this book, I realised how my now much-loved dog deserves to have a book dedicated to him. In many ways, he is the dog of my dreams. However, he is still a Border Collie, and I have learned not to put him in situations where he cannot cope. Movement is a trigger for him. Although he is now old and suffering from arthritis, he is still triggered to chase. I found this out last week when a flock of sheep appeared on the Malvern Hills while we were on a walking holiday. They took one look at Fred and began to run. Luckily, Fred was on a lead, but he suddenly lunged forward, to my surprise. I thought he was too old for such antics. But it helped me realise that a dog's working drive stays with them till their dying day. But we love him despite all the hardwired behaviours that caused me headaches when I first brought him home. Moreover, I have learned over the years, whilst training him, how to redirect his working drive. However, I wished someone had told me when I bought Fred how a dog with an intact work ethic would impact my life.

Yet, it was Fred who brought me into a dog training community that seeks to understand why any dog, working or otherwise, acts as they do. I can only be grateful for this, and my greatest desire for this book is that it will help other dog guardians like me struggling with their dog's antics. But some owners also grapple with dogs that seem disinterested in any activity—even a walk. So, if you have a dog like this or a run-of-the-mill pooch who has no working drive and is happy to be a couch potato, this book is still for you. For it is through my experiences with Fred I have come to understand how everyday interactions are essential for building a better bond with your dog.

Much has been written about the therapeutic benefits of a dog. The therapeutic effects of the dog have long been promoted for our mental and physical health. Still, it is a problem for this area of science to be entirely evidence-based driven, as it depends on many variables. The therapeutic relationship between dog and owner is very much dependent on the social relationships between family members and the temperament and character of each dog. A dog's personality, like people's, is hugely variable. We must understand that different breed types have different needs. By understanding what a dog needs, we can create a relationship with our dog that will benefit both the dog and us.

In the past, the owner or its breeding took the blame for the dog's poor behaviour. However, in my experience, most of the new guardians I meet have tried to understand the breed of their choice. But breed descriptions on the Internet are often misleading. They don't point out that these dogs have different motor patterns. From Chihuahuas to Great Danes, each dog is an individual with an impulse to behave differently. These behaviours might not fit your household.

To gather livestock, breeders use herding dogs like Fred, while hunting dogs are for flushing out and picking up shot birds for the hunter. Guardian dogs guard property and people, and Companion dogs are those toy breeds so famous for sitting on the knee to keep you warm. All of these dogs have a genotype that dictates their motor pattern. The problems come when these motor patterns clash with the dog's environment.

Beneath every cuddly ball of fluff is a genotype ready to kick-start the hardwiring within the dog. The dog then acts on the hardwiring for its entertainment, and a new owner may be shocked when their pup shows its true colours after a few weeks. The owner hoped training this cute bundle would be easy when they bought it from the breeder. They had swallowed the myths that good socialisation and 'good' breeding would give them what they wanted. They wanted a dog that showed undivided attention and devotion. In short, they wanted a dog that only appears in storybooks like *Lassie Come-Home*.

Over my working life, I have had the privilege of coming alongside many owners whilst running a veterinary practice. These clients have often told me that they did not fully comprehend the impact a puppy or new dog would have on their lives. After running dog training classes alongside my husband, I gained a unique perspective on a dog's guardianship. Furthermore, as a trained English and Drama teacher, I am interested in how the human condition reflects in stories. I realised that the stories we tell are integral to creating the right and healthy atmosphere for our relationship with a dog. The narrative we tell ourselves and others about our dogs will impact our behaviour and, in turn, influence our dogs' behaviour. If we start telling everyone we have made a mistake and our dog is 'the worst dog ever,' our demeanour will affect our dog. And our feelings will, in turn, affect our behaviour around them.

I am not saying you are the type who starts hitting your dog. But unfortunately, some owners still think a rolled-up newspaper is a suitable reprimand for a misdemeanour, or they may even resort to prong or shock collars. During my years in practice, I have come across well-meaning owners who have justified using such aversive methods. These clients believe it is the only way to save their dog's life. For example, for a dog that chases cars—the owner will use a shock collar to administer a bolt of electricity to the dog's neck when the owner presses a button. The dog is then startled into stopping the chase so the trainer can interrupt the unwanted behaviour. But using pain to interrupt behaviour is downright cruel and ineffective. There is proof that owners who often use this interrupter find that their dog links the punishment with them rather than the unwanted behaviour. Such a link can have disastrous consequences for the dog and owner, as the dog may show aggression towards the owner if they feel there is no means of escape. I have seen relationships with the dog irrevocably break down after such an event. There are much better ways of preventing a dog from chasing cars. It is so simple, really—a lead.

Most owners love their dogs and have been misled into carrying out harsh training methods. And unfortunately, there are still trainers instructing these desperate clients to carry out punitive methods to gain a dog's obedience. Therefore, as a culture, we must understand why punishment is such an attractive avenue for a dog owner to follow. In the heat of the moment, the temptation to administer punishment is strong. As human beings, we have a sense of shame (we do not want to be seen as owning the pariah of society). So, we feel that wrongdoing has to be punished. Also, smacking or any other outburst such as yanking on the lead, pinching ears, or just shouting at the dog may give immediate relief from our emotions. Therefore, as owners, we can dole out physical punishment out of fear and anger to change the dog's behaviour. But such actions inhibit curiosity as to why the dog is doing that behaviour in the first place.

I would encourage owners to understand themselves and how their emotions affect their dogs. When we lose our temper with our dogs, the dog's amygdala will create an automatic response to give flight or fight. Even if you are the kindest person on the planet, your body language and tone of voice show your view of your dog. The dog will know you are displeased and will either try to escape and run away at every opportunity they get or act like a clown. And if those tactics do not work and you corner them, they might take more drastic measures to show that they are unhappy. The trick is to know how your dog is feeling and guide them to make more appropriate choices, a skill which I call dogmanship.

Dogmanship is a term I first used in my book *In Search of Lassie* to describe competent dog trainers with skilled dog insight. Because of Fred, I made my own journey to good dogmanship; I learned how to train working dogs in the urban environment to fulfil their breed needs. I would not recommend such a combination of a working dog and an urban family house. Still, as everyday dog owners, many of us have had to deal with this predicament as dog breeders have asserted that their dog would make a good pet. This reassurance is often misleading. Their dog breed may very well make an excellent pet. However, they fail to inform the new owner how to obtain such a promise. This book looks to rectify this.

***

In Part I, I will endeavour to help the reader to rediscover joy with their dog. Joy is often elusive because of broken expectations you built before acquiring your puppy or rescue dog.

J–Join Your Dream with Reality

We bring a dog into our family home, hoping for the perfect relationship. If our dogs begin to misbehave, we look to fix them. However, as guardians of our puppy's or rescue dog's future, we must make a paradigm shift in understanding.

We must move away from functional dog training and link our 'powerful why' with the outcomes we are looking for with our dog. Such an approach means we need to understand ourselves and permit ourselves to question why dog training has not as yet worked for us.

Our dogs uniquely experience their environment, and their individual needs may clash with your lifestyle. Its breed type dictates each of its needs. Furthermore, the environmental experience, previous relationships with people, other dogs, and any other pet in its early years will dictate reactions. Therefore, it is essential to know your breeder's approach to dogs and the raising of puppies. You may be feeling stressed and overwhelmed by the enormity of the task that lies before you as you come to understand some of the fundamental mistakes that every new owner makes. But there is hope; you can settle your dog into a daily game-planned schedule that restores harmony to your household.

O–Overcoming the Roadblocks to Your Dreams

In Part I, I will focus on our emotional responses to the stress that your dog might be causing you and how we might change the story for a better one. After all, we all want a paragon of virtue and not have our dog seen as a neighbourhood pariah with people walking across the street to avoid us. In short, we want our dogs to be good citizens. In this book section, I unwrap how we can change our mindset to create the right atmosphere for our dogs to learn to live with us in harmony.

Y–Yes, to Daily Games That Make a Difference.

I believe true joy is found by seeking to build a relationship with the dog so we can connect our dream to the reality of the dog we own. Therefore, my book endeavours to join the joy with the dog you have in front of you. By failing to join the concept of the dog's environment and breed needs to the dog's breed type, plus its ability to learn to cope with the pressures of our urban lives, your relationship with your dog may irrevocably break down. I want to spare any new owner the pain of that experience. Choose suitable games in this book to discover how to mend your relationship with your dog. We must understand that the **J**oy of dog ownership can only happen when we can **O**vercome the roadblocks to our aspirations by saying **Y**es to daily games. These games will make all the difference to our dog's interpretation and reaction to its environment.

***

In Part II, I will discuss how every **D**og is on a mission, and when **O**ut and about, we have to consider how their breed needs should inform our training. I will also show how **Game** plans lead to a dog of your dreams—albeit with the quirks that come along with its breed type and parentage. With my own Leonberger, I have learned to work with her guarding and hunting instincts rather than trying to work against them. And in many ways, I came to be grateful for them as she barked ferociously at the burglar who attempted to access our veterinary surgery in search of drugs.

Using the acronym D.O.G., I unwrap the most persistent problems every new dog owner must face.

D—Dog on a Mission

Every dog has a mission, which is hardwired through its breeding. One of the Companion dog's missions is to get as close to you as possible due to its breed's origins. For example, Companion dogs, bred to be loyal lap dogs, find it challenging to be separated from their owners. And we all will experience this with new puppies; we cannot help but be upset by the whimperings of the first night when we get the puppy home. Biting comes next, including puppy biting and resource guarding (nipping at the owner when they do not want to give up a stolen item). During the evolution of the dog, we have selectively bred the hunting dog to enhance possessive behaviour. The need for a dog to hold game birds was helpful to us as we utilised the behaviour for our hunting purposes. However, now when our working cocker possesses an object, we must remember that relinquishing any item in its mouth must be taught. We must not be surprised when they refuse to let go of the article, for it was a human being who sought and bred for this behaviour in the first place. It is not 'bad' behaviour. And if the dog aggresses towards us, this resource guarding happens because we as humans have taught them that we are unsafe and will steal valuable items from them.

O—Out and About—Training for the Situation, Not in the Situation

When we leave the front door, our dogs become so excited they will be tempted to jump up at strangers and pull on their lead or not come back when called. The recall and walking on the lead should always be thought of as one and the same. Many owners train the walking on the leash before establishing a 'good recall,' not realising that leash walking is a prolonged recall. As you negotiate these training issues, I will endeavour to change your view of how a dog thinks and learns. It is better to train for the situation than when the problems occur.

G—Game Plans—Understanding That Dog Training Is 24/7

It is now accepted that our dogs have emotions and that our own emotions can react to what seems to be defiance, which can cause a breakdown in the relationship. I want every dog owner to resist seeing unwanted behaviours as confirmation that the dog is 'bad'— the unspoken fear of many a dog owner. Rather than having an emotional response, I encourage you to study your dog's reactions to find solutions. I will endeavour to show that these solutions will be seen by playing games with your dog, which is fun for you and the dog. In the back of the book, you will find game-plan vision worksheets to help you develop a relationship with the dog you always wanted. We teach our dogs every moment of the day, and I hope to show an owner through my game plans how they can be intentional about what they teach.

***

In conclusion, I discuss why it is so vital that we address the issues of dog ownership. Our dogs have nowhere else they can live, as the human world is a dog's natural environment. Without us, the Canis familiaris could become an endangered species. So come with me on your journey of doggy enlightenment and understand what it is to be a dog. Today there are far more instances of aggression, either towards another dog or person. By following my game-plan vision worksheets, I hope to prevent such problems. Dogs can reach their true potential with the right approach of 24/7 game training, where every event in their lives is seen as a possibility for a learning experience. And for us, at the other end of the lead, we can achieve the true joy of owning the dog of our dreams.

PART I: WHAT IT IS TO BE HUMAN

Many dog training books start with the subject of the functional training of a dog. For example, how to get a dog to sit, stay, and lie down, etc. They might also dive into how dogs learn and canine ethology—the study of dog behaviour. However, I believe that we must first look at ourselves before training a dog. When we own a dog, we become a part of a team: the dog and us. Our dogs look to us for leadership, and in all good leadership research, it has been proven that the best leaders are those who have learned to be leaders in their personal lives.

Like anything in life, we have to make a plan for outcomes if we want to succeed. So many clients say they can't find time to fit in training for their dogs. They have a puppy, but their elderly parent is taken to hospital. Their children are taking exams whilst they are in the middle of remodelling their kitchen. Where is the time to be found? I sympathise because I do understand how they feel. Yes, I have been there, too, but I have also learned that we can become victims of circumstances in our lives or overcomers.

So many things can get in the way of you carrying out your goals, and you might even wonder if your life is going the way you want it to go. After realising that my life was drifting in the wrong direction, I learned to say "Yes" to planning. I realised planning was not only essential for my daily tasks and goals but was also essential for my writing and my dog training goals. For example, I want to write several books, train my dogs, volunteer as a trainer for Dog A.I.D., help with grandchildren, plus remodel my house.[1] Now any of these things on my list could slide off the radar. I might say: "I'll get around to writing that book one day." However, because I am caught up with many daily tasks, I will never get around to writing unless I plan. And the same goes for training my dogs; if I don't plan, their training will drift. I probably would get away with it if I had an ordinary run-of-the-mill pet dog, but I cannot afford to be slapdash with an over fifty kg guarding breed. You, too, may realise that something has to be done with your dog, as it has become unruly. Or you may have a pet dog who seems okay, but you were hoping for more. How will planning make a breakthrough in realising your original dreams when you first got your dog?

---

[1] *Dog A.I.D (Assistance in Disability) is a charity which helps train pet dogs to become fully qualified Assistance Dogs. The charity assists people with physical disabilities by helping them train their own dogs to complete everyday tasks and, in some circumstances, provide life-saving interventions.*

When looking back on my life, I realised that I often played the victim. I have said: "I can't possibly do this or that until I have more time or if circumstances are different (the things of importance have changed over the years)." And for my dogs, I have said that they can't do this or that because they don't like toys or they don't like food. Yes, I have been where many new owners are right now. I have even been envious of compliant Labrador owners whose dog seems only too happy to please. Or I played the villain by saying I'm so rubbish at organising and planning. I can never find the time. Or I can never be as good at training as Susan Garrett (one of the most successful dog trainers and agility competitors internationally known for her dogmanship). I have not had the years of competitive skills she has had. Whichever mindset I chose, circumstances always got the upper hand. However, I have always loved stories and have been an avid reader from a young age. I particularly loved real stories about real people's struggles in their lives. Indeed, the Victorian writer, Lord Thomas Macaulay, wrote after the death of his much-loved sister, "that I have not utterly sunk under this blow, I owe chiefly to literature. Literature has saved my life and my reason."[2] By sharing stories, we understand that we are not alone. We all share in one common humanity with universal truths. And it is because I discovered the universal truths of

---

[2] *Macaulay, Thomas. The History of England. Edited and abridged by Hugh Trevor-Roper. London : Penguin Books, 1968 p.334*

dog ownership that I created my vision game plans. With these game plans, dear reader, you, too, can create a new storyline with your dog and discover joy along the way.

Stories give narrative traction to a better future. Choosing our words to report on our past dog-owning experiences increases our understanding. I would also encourage my readers to seek books about other dog-owner experiences. By reading people's stories about dog-owning challenges, we will understand the universal truths of dog guardianship. Stories engage with our emotions, and when we write our own stories, we gain a new perspective on our problems, sorrows and joys. The latest research has shown that remapping an account of your life and adding a new ending can lead to outcomes that you thought were impossible.[3] We can indeed plan to make our dreams a reality—detailed planning for both personal goals and goals for our dogs.

Here, I would ask you, dear reader, to be patient with yourself and your dog. If you have a naughty or nervous dog, you are probably chomping at the bit to know how to get your dog to calm down. And you might want to focus on the functional aspect of dog training, such as not jumping up, etc. However, dog training issues are often caused by the dog's

---

[3] *"Writing to Awaken: Writing Studies." Mark Matousek, July 8, 2021.*
   https://markmatousek.com/books/writing-to-awaken-book/writing-studies/.

emotional responses to their environment and you as their guardian. So, my most significant piece of advice to new dog owners is to know yourself. You might reply, "I just want to enjoy my dog without all the *who-ha* attached to it." I find that it is not unusual for clients to react to me as they might if someone suggested they might need to see a psychiatrist. Saying that you or your dog needs psychiatric help is a threatening prospect. No one wants to feel judged. And that is what it is to be human.

We prefer to learn how to train a dog to sit, stay, or come back rather than understand why our dogs do the things we do not want them to do. We want to stop our dogs from barking or lunging because it is embarrassing for us. But often, we need to understand why the dog is doing that in the first place. Many owners take their dogs to dog training classes to stop these behaviours, fearing that their dogs will become fearful and show dog-on-dog aggression. However, the dog training class is where your dog will practise the behaviour you do not want.

I am not saying training or training classes are wrong. I belong to a dog training club myself. However, a blanket approach to functional training to try and stop your dog from lunging or barking fearfully on the end of the lead will not work. Instead, we must teach a rescue dog or puppy to be resilient before even taking our dog to training classes. Resilience training should start when you bring your rescue dog or puppy home. A puppy needs to be fully vaccinated before joining a class anyway. You can use this time to socialise with people and other dogs (carefully chosen for their temperament) and habituate your dog to its new environment. Whether you have a puppy or an adult dog from a rescue centre, I recommend my games to build a bond with your dog and build up your dog's resilience. And by following the Game plans, you will discover the joy of dog ownership. Whatever background your dog comes from, I promise the vision plans will help all dogs.

Chapter 1

JOIN THE
DREAM WITH THE REALITY

So you have bought a pup or adopted a dog from a rescue kennel. Whatever the case, you are now facing reality. After the first few weeks, your dog's honeymoon period has ended. You are now finding that your dog is annoying you. Your dog is showing you its true colours and may have pinched your socks and run into the garden with them. Or your dog has even swallowed the socks as you tried to retrieve them, causing you to pay a massive vet bill.[4] It is now, when the honeymoon period has ended, that we need to understand ourselves and why we bought or rescued a dog in the first place.

---

[4] *Removing a foreign object from a dog's stomach is an expensive business. Don't blame the vet; it is a complicated operation that needs the attention of many staff, medication and time, so it all adds up.*

Knowing Your Powerful Why

First of all, know your 'powerful why' for getting your dog in the first place. The reasons why people buy a dog are varied as people's lives, and motivations are varied. We all have a reason for purchasing a pup or rescuing a dog. But, when we lose sight of what that why was, we will also lose the motivation to take on intentional training for our dogs. We will allow the drift to occur, and whether we realise it or not, we teach our dogs something every day. Sometimes, without our knowledge, our dogs make us jump through the hoops rather than the other way around.

You may have been one of many who dream of rescuing a feral dog you have seen on holiday and have approached one of their rescue centres. There is something very satisfying about the idea of saving an animal. However, as a word of caution, Carri Westgarth, a research fellow in human-animal interactions at the University of Liverpool, believes the demand for adoption of dogs from overseas results in a potential for unscrupulous breeding practices. She suggests puppy farms may be breeding 'street dogs' to satisfy this demand.[5]

Why, then, are we drawn to look to save another species? I believe these breeders are cashing in on the human need to

---

[5] *Why are we adopting so many dogs from abroad Loeb, Josh, 2018,* **Vet Record**, *Vol. 183, p.615.*

fix and find meaning in this disjointed and fragmented world of disconnection. Indeed, the biologist E. O. Wilson hypothesised that our species has an instinctive affiliation with the natural world. Hal Herzog often proves this trait known as biophilia by including pictures of kittens and puppies in his talks, which usually evoke a chorus of "oohs and ahhs" from his audience. Thus the audience demonstrates humans' natural attraction towards caregiving to species other than ours.[6]

Science has explained our attraction to bringing another species into our homes. Still, you may have a simple dream that your new puppy will be your companion after a day at work. But instead, your dog paws at your sleeves and whines. Your dog may even constantly drop the ball in your lap. All these 'action prompting' activities happen when you just want to sit in front of the T.V. to veg out after a hard day. Yet to your utter frustration, your dog has decided it is time to play.

You may have just bought a puppy in the hope that it will show its gratitude with unswerving devotion. However, it has chased the neighbour's cat and chewed holes in your skirting boards and walls. Or you may have dreamed of taking your new dog for a daily jog around the park. Still, your dog chooses to bomb off to visit with another dog and not take a blind bit of notice to your shouts for him to come back.

---

[6] *Herzog, Hal. Some We Love, Some We Hate, Some We Eat: Why it's so Hard to Think Straight About Animals (P.S). e-book. Sidney: HarperCollins e-books, 2010 p. 39.*

Whatever the case, now your dreams are shattered by your dog acting up, and you wonder if you should have got the dog in the first place because it isn't working out as you had hoped.

Regrettably, one in ten people in the UK relinquishes their pup in the first month of buying their dog. Over 54% said they knew they had made a mistake after getting the dog home, and over a quarter had realised that looking after a puppy was as hard as having a newborn.[7] And sadly, those relinquished to rescue centres are often returned due to the new owner's inability to cope with the rescued dog's antics. Almost twenty per cent of adopted dogs have already been rehomed once before. The reason often for the return to the rehoming centre is the new owner said they could not cope with the dog's behaviour.[8] So, how can the relinquishment of dogs be prevented, and how can you find the energy to recommit to bringing harmony back to your household?

Understanding Yourself

When the relationship with your new dog has broken down, you need to reconnect with your 'powerful why.' However, most of those who relinquish their dog have lost touch with

---

[7] Pacelli, Alessandra, (2018, March 22) One in ten puppies given up after a month in UK. www.dogstodaymagazine.co.uk/2018/03/22/one-ten-puppies-given-month-uk-research-says/

[8] Team, Pets4Homes Editorial. "Canine Rehoming and Its Failure Rate." Pets4Homes, March 21, 2022. https://www.pets4homes.co.uk/pet-advice/canine-rehoming-and-its-failure-rate.html.

their original dream. The dream is not strong enough, and the new owner begins to listen to the naysayers of this world. How, then, can a new dog owner rekindle their powerful why? It takes guts and the ability to laugh at yourself. Your 'why' needs to be strong enough to overcome the victim or villain mentality. In short, you need to understand yourself and become the hero in the new story about your dog. You need to have a growth mindset and push beyond your comfort zone.

Give Yourself Permission

In the past, the 'what' of dog training has focused on the functional sit or lie down etc. But, this training has failed to focus on the 'why.' The 'why' is inspirational rather than functional. Asking 'why' separates us from achievement and success, for achievement measured by your dog's behaviour may not always align with your 'powerful why.' You may achieve a good sit or recall (coming back when called) in a dog training class, but on a walk, your dog still bombs off to the other end of the field to visit another dog and is deaf to your calls. Instead of getting cross, we can get curious. When you ask 'why,' you will find inspiration to solve your dog training struggles. It helps us keep going even when our dogs act like delinquent teenagers.

When we were kids, we constantly asked our parents, 'why?' Unfortunately, we seem to have lost our childhood curiosity. We accept other people's opinions without question, and we do not challenge the thinking of others. Unfortunately, dog training professionals are unregulated, and we may be given poor advice. Permit yourself to question how things stand and ask yourself 'why' it should be done that way, especially if you are advised to use harsh methods to show your dog who is boss. Suppose you are a person who thinks about the 'why' of the training methods you employ rather than 'what' is done for a given situation in your dog's life. In that case, you are more likely to find a kinder and more innovative answer to your problem. Therefore, you are more likely to find a solution. 'Why?' is the most fantastic question to ask when you come across the roadblocks to your dog becoming the dog you always wanted. Ask yourself, *Why is my dog doing this?* And if you don't know the answer, then it is time to seek a dog training professional you can trust.

With a trained professional, you can collaborate to ask why your dog is doing the things they do—asking 'why' is powerful because it helps you link where you are now with what you want. It brings clarity to the complexity that is both you and your dog. You will experience those ah-ha moments that strengthen your relationship with your dog. You will come to grips with your motivations and understand how to solve problems that arise. Dog ownership is a complex topic, and sometimes when you experience those moments of clarity, everything begins to fit together to create the dog you always wanted. And along the way, you will learn so much more about yourself. Indeed, I believe our relationship with our dog helps us become more human.

Chapter 2

OVERCOMING THE ROADBLOCKS

To build a relationship with our dogs, we must transfer the value of what they want to **US**. The aim is not to be the gatekeeper of what they want; instead, they see us as the key to all that is good in life. We provide the leadership they need. As the human in the equation, the trick is to evaluate your dog's values. When we take what he wants and transfer that to what we would like, we move our dog's energy in the right direction. For example, if your dog is trying to pull you on his lead to get to the park, we must stop and ask him to walk calmly for a few paces, then reward him with the park run. Therefore, using the Premack principle, allowing a dog to go for a free run after insisting your dog walks calmly to the park will reinforce the loose leash walking.[9] The Premack principle is sometimes called the 'grandma's rule' or first/then. Because at Grandma's, you must first eat your dinner and then get a cookie. As a grandma, I find it challenging to keep to that rule. And so do many of my clients who allow their dogs to pull them to the park. A dog only carries out a behaviour he has practised and finds rewarding. So, if we allow our dogs to pull us to the park, the free run will reinforce that behaviour too. But it is no good feeling that we have to punish that naughty behaviour. Because we are humans, we desire to have the dog suffer the consequences of its actions. Only the other day, I heard a man talking to his dog. "No," he said whilst yanking him on the lead, "you don't get the cookie till you learn to behave." But dogs do not understand complete sentences. His owner thought his dog was being 'stubborn.' However, he did not comprehend how dogs think or learn. The dog's owner needed to make a paradigm shift in his thinking. Rather than chastising the dog, which only made him act up, he needed to understand what the dog wanted. Then, by allowing him that reward straight after he practised walking nicely, he would find his dog would have happily complied. His constant corrections with the yank on the collar with the lead only

---

[9] *David Premack was an American psychologist whose work reinforces what we know about behaviour and cognition.*

revved up his dog even more. His shouts of "heel" had become a poisoned cue.

You only attach a cue to an established behaviour that is correctly carried out. It is a bit like programming a computer. Rubbish in, and there will be rubbish out. A cue becomes poisoned if it is linked with you nagging the dog to do something, whilst it completely ignores the cue. If you allow your dog to choose to stay by your side because it will get your dog a valued reward, then your dog will never think to pull on the lead again.[10] My dogs stay by my side until I give them a release cue, such as 'free.'

Therefore, we can overcome roadblocks to our dogs' training from the stance of benevolent leaders. Consequently, I believe our dogs teach us to be kinder human beings. Our dogs can also allow us to live more courageously if we open ourselves up to new ideas. Indeed, it has been said that we cannot lead others until we have learned to lead ourselves. We must overcome our need to punish behaviour we do not want—equally valid for raising children or managing a busy office.

As a practice manager for a busy veterinary practice, I know too well how losing your cool does not help your team's performance. The same is true of dog training, for you and

---

[10] *See loose leash games*

your dog are a team. Therefore, I always advise clients not to train their dogs if they feel tired or unwell. Instead, sit down and plan how you want to go forward. Give yourself and your dog a break, and start again when you feel more optimistic.

A Roadblock Is a Pointer, Not a Disappointment.

First, we need to take a paradigm shift in seeing that a roadblock is a pointer towards success and not just a disappointment. As a teacher, I was taught at university the importance of evaluation. Indeed, I often advise clients to film themselves when working through my game plans. Then they will see clearly what their roadblock might be. When we look at a roadblock in the training of our dogs, we can use them to gain clarity as to what we need to do in the future, and they help us see measurable progress. However, I must make a caveat here, as humans can become highly motivated by ambition and a sense of competition. These motives can become toxic if we become obsessed purely with the functional abilities of our dog rather than concentrating on the relationship with our dog first and foremost. I would love to see more relationship-building exercises in our dog clubs today. Sadly, we often just put them through a schedule of functional drilling of desired behaviours without understanding their reactions.

We do not consider the dog's emotions in the situation, and many owners do not even recognise their dog's body language; in their own way, their dogs are screaming out for help. However, the dog guardian faced with a barking dog or a dog biting them in sheer frustration is at a loss as they seek to control their dog in a dog club training session. In many ways being in a dog training class is the wrong place for them. It would be better if owners were taught the mechanics of dog training first—more about that in Part II. However, we need to understand our emotions too. Often, a dog owner knows that their puppy is having a problem and just wants to fix their dog. But dogs, like humans, are all individuals with their own likes and dislikes. On our journey of doggy enlightenment, we must understand that the journey is as important as our final destination. It is a bit like guardians standing at the school fence discussing how quickly their child has learned to read. I have two grown-up children making their own way in the world, so I realise how unproductive those conversations were. Teaching our children the joy of reading instead of thinking about the functional level they attained would have been far more productive.

Failing Forward

There will always be times when you fail, and your dog will misbehave. Like children, dogs are not perfect. The myth of the perfect dog only belongs to story books. However, in my experience, the guilt and anger associated with an owner coming to terms with a badly-behaved dog can be directed internally. As James O'Heare points out, owners 'can obsess about what they did wrong and what they could have done better. They may feel like they have let their friend down, not having socialised him enough or trained him well. They may also experience grief for the loss of the bond of their companion.' O'Heare explains how this grief can cause embarrassment as they believe their dog's behaviour reflects badly on them, and the grief can cause anger, which is then directed at others or even towards the dog.[11] I believe, like a failed dieter, a dog guardian has to decide what they want and look for new ways of doing things.

As the saying goes, "to err is human to forgive is divine."[12] Dogs are so good at forgetting what has passed. I am surprised how ready they are to show affection towards an owner who regularly doles out punishment, which may be a yank on the lead to a smack on the nose. They are so ready to forgive and teach us how to be better humans.

In her book, *Animal Grace*, Mary Lou Randour explains how our relationship with animals 'allows us … to gain a spiritual advantage,' as they 'offer us a unique opportunity to transcend the boundaries of our human perspectives, they allow us to stretch our consciousness toward understanding what it is like to be different. This stretching enables us to

---

[11] *O'Heare, James. Aggressive Behaviour in Dogs. Canada: Dogpsych Publishing, 2007 p.31.*
[12] *"To err is human, to forgive is divine", is a quote from Alexander Pope who is known as one of the greatest English poets.*

grow beyond our narrow viewpoint.' She asks, 'How can we possibly appreciate and move toward spiritual wholeness if we cannot see beyond our species? How can we come to know God, or grasp the interconnectedness of all life, if we limit ourselves to knowing only our own kind?' Then, she concludes, 'The goal of compassion is not to care because someone is like us but to care because they are themselves.'[13] So when we show genuine compassion for our dogs, we can gain a new viewpoint on our struggles with relationships and loss. Owning my dogs has taught me a great deal about letting things go and not being trapped in a cycle of telling and retelling unbeneficial stories. Indeed, I have to forgive my dogs as well as myself before I can move forward.

Only the other day, I was shocked by my Leonberger's behaviour. And to be honest, I was both embarrassed and burdened with feelings of guilt—all completely unhelpful emotions. So when my husband and I found ourselves rehearsing a negative story, we decided it would be better to own up to our feelings. We decided to bring them into the light to deal with them appropriately. I told Robert how angry I felt towards the other dog owner. "She could see I was struggling to hold my fifty kg dog, yet she kept coming. If she had stopped, I could have brought Joy's focus back," I complained.

---

[13] Randour, Mary Lou. Animal Grace. Kindle. California : New World Livrary, 2000 p.6.

Joy is seven years old, highly trained, and goes to a weekly dog club where she shows no aggression to other dogs. I realised guilt was making me feel the shame of my lack of control over her, and when we feel shame, we often blame others. Then we spoke about the lack of education for the ordinary dog owner and how instruction is rarely given about how dog owners should negotiate with other dog owners on a walk. My seven-year-old dog had been taught to weave politely around other dogs. Still, the other dog triggered a fear response in the woods, where a dog had previously set on her. I then heard in my head: *Call yourself a dog trainer!* The whispered criticism inside our heads accompanies the imposter syndrome, a familiar feeling amongst many professionals.

The belief that all dog trainers should have perfectly behaved dogs must be debunked now. If you have a trainer who does not know how to deal with failure, run a mile. They will not be able to empathise with your predicament. In the main, it is only because of their failures that they can be the sherpa for future dog owners. They have been up that mountain and have come down again. They appreciate another dog owner's pain and want to help. They will completely understand how you might feel resentment towards your dog. They will have had to fight their own emotions to come through the other side. They know that as humans, we all fail, but we can also fail forward. They realise that the failure is a pointer towards taking action. They then decide what necessary action they need to take. For me, it is evaluating Joy's alarm bark was situational. The other dog sparked memories of a past attack, and I have decided to give those particular woods a miss for the time being. I will also practise the game 'this way' for the next three weeks.

As I tell my clients, dogs are dogs. We cannot resent a normal dog's behaviour. I have set out here to be honest about how things can unexpectedly go wrong for any handler. So please, fellow dog owners, always give other dog owners space. And please, please do not judge other dog owners poorly. When we own a dog, forgiveness is a skill that we become better at if we only give ourselves, our dogs, and others the grace they deserve. Our mistakes can turn our past struggles into growth opportunities.

Hope Deferred Makes the Heart Sick[14]

I often ask people who have attended my dog training classes about their hopes for their puppy. Most owners quote a list of attributes such as being confident and able to be taken most places. They should be energetic and go running with them. Still, they must be friendly and approachable with strangers and other dogs on their excursions. They must be intelligent, but at the same time, heaven forbid they should bark at the

---

[14] *Proverbs 13:12*

neighbour through the fence or poop on the communal front lawn. Jon Katz points out that dogs that 'act like well-behaved humans—are perceived more positively by their owners. "Actual" dogs—who behave more like dogs—generate much lower levels of affection from their owners.' [15]

I am only human and have had to admit that I resented Joy for showing me up when she barked at the dog in the woods. I probably feared the judgement of the other owner. When Joy is more herself, she trots gracefully by my side, and my heart wells up with pride. The desire for a saintly dog, just like Lassie, has always been there since childhood, even though I know today it is an unrealistic expectation. That day my heart felt sick with guilt as Joy failed to live up to what I had hoped. I long for her to be all she can be, an ambassador for the large breed of Guardian dog that is often feared. However, that day she did not live up to my hopes. Many readers will find that their dog does not always live up to theirs. All these high expectations are bound to lead to a broken relationship with our dogs; no dog can be a paragon of virtue. Unfortunately, we expect more from our dogs than we do from a child.

Many clients have contacted me because they have experienced the disappointment of broken expectations. They have hoped for so much. But they have had to face the reality

---

[15] *Katz, Jon. The New Work of Dogs: Tending to Life, Love and Family. Kindle. New York: Villard, 2003 p.212.*

of the dog in front of them. And like me, the most disappointing situation for an owner is when their dog barks and lunges at other dogs, or even worse, they have got into a dog fight. When Joy was attacked, to my surprise, she did not fight back and was severely bitten and needed antibiotics. I would be shocked if her intentions were to fight when she decided to lunge and bark at the other dog. But I was not going to let go. I was not going to risk it. I did eventually get her focus back. But as I tell my clients who have gone through a similar experience: Both you and your dog will need at least seventy-two hours to get over the incident before attempting to go for a walk again. In the meantime, play games with your dog to rebuild your faith in them and yourself.

For all of us, a dog attacking our dog can be a frightening experience. We do not talk enough about how such encounters affect us. Sometimes it is difficult to admit to someone that you are feeling anxious about going on future walks with your dog. I know clients who have gone through some harrowing experiences with their dogs. In effect, they have post-traumatic stress disorder (PTSD). As a result, their dog becomes nervous too. The anxious cycle is often exacerbated by the fact that the dog has a propensity to be shy in the first place. Therefore, the dog becomes super vigilant as they sense their owner's worry about what might be coming around the corner. So, if you have had your dog attacked and find it challenging to take your dog out on a walk again without breaking out in a cold sweat, it is time to seek help. I would suggest you seek professional support for yourself and your dog. You might find the experience will be turned to your benefit as you reach out for help.

As humans, we were made for connection. Although the connection with a dog may stretch you, the relationship will also help you grow. When we seek authentic relationships with each other and the animals that live alongside us, we will find life. A life full of fun and games will gladden the heart and improve our dogs' mental health and our own mood. We then will fulfil the heart's desire—to own the dog of our dreams. A dog just like Lassie. As Proverbs 13:12 says: 'Hope deferred makes the heart sick, but a longing fulfilled is a tree of life.'

Chapter 3

YES, TO GAME PLANS

Me Human—You Dog

We would all love to believe our dogs do things because they love us. The other day I was listening to my friends chatting during our pottery class. My ears pricked as I heard them talking about how their dogs were nothing like Lassie. "Yes," said one friend as she laughed, "I walk in our local woods, and if I fell, there would be no one for miles to help me. My dog would probably just smack me in the face with their paw as if to say, "Get up, silly woman." I don't think there would be any chance she would run and find help." My friend's banter revealed her disappointment with her dog for not living up to the storybook version of a dog.

The heroic dog emblem has been a long tradition in literature. In fact, Eric Knight purloined his story, *Lassie Come-Home*, from Elizabeth Gaskell's tale of a hero dog of the same name who was sent back to get help for two brothers lost in the snow. Like Gaskell, in *The Half-Brothers* (1859), Knight follows the convention where the dog is used as a symbol of loyalty. Such loyalty is part of folklore that goes far back into man's history. Humankind from early times has shown 'awareness of the ancient intelligence of the dog, his sense of unity with the dog, and recognition of the mystery of his spirit.' Before books, the oral tradition of telling and retelling stories helped man comprehend their place in the world. In these stories, a dog often accompanied deities who appeared as a go-between, protector, or culture hero (fire bringer, food bringer, even man bringer in a few instances).[16] The idea of redemption brought to us by a dog is even perpetuated by news stories of today, especially whilst our culture is battling with generalised anxieties caused by pandemics and climate change. Stories of dogs giving solace to owners are highly topical. The culture proliferates the idea that although we might be gripped by fears of mortality and being isolated from our fellow man, we can find a friend in a dog.

Yes, in general, dogs can be that friend. And when we are allowed to interact freely with our fellow man, dogs can act as a social lubricant. Talking about your dog breaks down barriers; even Eric Knight recognised this in his story *Lassie Come-Home*. However, as I argue in my book, *In Search of*

---

[16] Leach, M. *God Had a Dog: Folklore of the Dog: Rutgers University Press, 1961 p.xi.*

Lassie: A Dog Owner's Guide to the Lassie Myth, the dog has been deified. We are treating our dogs inappropriately and expect too much from them. Dogs showing actual dog behaviour incur our disappointment and, in some cases, our anger. All because Walt Disney seized on Knight's story after seeing the opportunity to cash in on the idea of the heroic dog.

When our dogs fail to live up to the Hollywood version of a dog, we may laugh, like my two friends, as there are no significant consequences. But, as Knight might say, "Any of 'em can turn bad," then we may be tempted to dole out punishment.[17] Much as you would punish a child for a misdemeanour. But even today, we are recognising how the discipline of children is outdated, and far more is achieved by using positive approaches to a child's education. Reinforcement of good behaviour is now understood to have more significant benefits to a child's outlook on life. So, I would advocate positive approaches to dog training. We now understand that dogs carry out specific behaviours because they are reinforced. Through the work of B. F. Skinner, an American psychologist and behaviourist of Harvard University (1958–1974), we now understand the importance of how behaviour can be affected by the environment. Indeed, our dogs constantly do two things as they engage with their

---

[17] Knight, Eric. *Lassie Come-Home. 75th Anniversary Edition.* New York City U.S.: Henry Holdt and Company ebook, 2015 p.123

environment: seeking pleasure or avoiding pain and discomfort. As humans, we tell ourselves stories to understand our world. Still, a dog is unable to project the consequences of his actions. He does not think about life and how his life is impacting its owners. A dog lives in that moment. They react at that moment to the environment. A dog will either avoid the pain or enjoy the pleasure.

Sometimes it is a behaviour we do not want. For example, kitchen counter surfing, where a dog's nose goes along the kitchen units until your dog spies your, or should I say, *smells* your sandwich. Gobble! It is gone, and that behaviour is reinforced because the kitchen counter was so kind as to dispense such lovely snacks. This behaviour is conditioned. So now we must understand how we can condition our dogs to do what we want them to do.

The Science of Communication

B.F. Skinner worked on conditioning. Skinner found the cross-over from classical conditioning to operant conditioning. This science stuff is important. We might not like to realise it, but we are all (both humans and dogs) a product of our conditioning. When you understand your reactions to environmental stimuli, you can understand how this will impact your dog's reactions. Understanding this will help to build the relationship with your dog you always wanted.

Classical conditioning is the learning that Pavlov's dogs showed.[18] Every time the dogs heard a bell, they got food, and pretty soon, they salivated when the bell rang, even when food was not present. Operant conditioning is linked with a consequence, i.e., pressing a lever and food is dispensed. Then there is a likelihood of the behaviour being repeated when the lever again is present. The dog will voluntarily choose the behaviour to produce the consequence—the food being dispensed. So how do we create the cross-over behaviour that we want? Skinner found that by using a clicker (a small box that makes a clicking noise when pressed), he could make the bridge between classical conditioning to operant conditioning.

When the click is made and food is dispensed, you can teach behaviour and indicate it is the correct behaviour with a click, and the dog knows that food will follow. I like the analogy that it's like taking a photograph, as you click as if trying to capture the moment. Every time you see your dog do anything, you can click the box and give a treat, which means your dog is more likely to produce the behaviour again. I did my research with this and clicked every time my border collie, Fred, twitched his ear. Once he caught onto why he was being clicked and rewarded for that behaviour, he repeated it. Some people find juggling food treats and clickers difficult, so I

---

[18] *Ivan Pavlov (1849–1936) is best known as the founder of behaviour therapy with his research into classical conditioning.*

suggest that these clients either use a clicker word such as 'yes' or they make a clicking noise with their mouth. Either way works. But whichever you choose, it immediately establishes a clear line of communication with your dog. Your dog will know how to get the reinforcing treats from you by behaving just as you asked.

Despite our ability to use operant conditioning, we now understand more about what might happen in a dog's brain. Therefore, as I have pointed out earlier, we should not concentrate only on the functional behaviour of our dogs and think of ways in which we might control them. We need to take a more compassionate approach to our dogs. I believe dog guardians cannot rely on classical and operant conditioning to manage dogs indiscriminately. We must look at how our dogs can or cannot cope with their environment. For example, we need to understand a dog barking in dog class or biting its owner out of fear or frustration needs to be both comforted for fear and given an outlet for its emotions, rather than be punished. We should now be thinking and learning as a human and dog team. And as the more evolved of the two species, we can take notice of the situation we are in and how our dogs may be reacting to that environment.

From the work of Gregory Berns, we now understand much more about how a dog learns. Berns carried out an experiment that showed how dogs could delay gratification, as the famous marshmallow experiment showed how children could do the same. However, the children in the famous experiment showed different ability levels, just as dogs in Berns's research showed different levels. In the M.R.I scanner, the dogs were asked to wait, and the scanner showed that the prefrontal lobe became active. The dogs with more activity in that area of their brain did much better in the experiment. But what was most surprising from the tests was that sometimes the dog was given a hot dog, and other times they were given praise only. When their responses in the rewards centre of their brains were looked at, in most cases, the dogs responded equally to praise and food. Berns's work shows that when we increase our dog's confidence, we are more likely to build relationships we always wanted. This research shows how much more we need to be involved in our relationship with our dogs.

Interestingly, Canine Companions wanted Berns to see which puppies were more likely to succeed as service dogs. After scanning the selected puppies, they found the best candidates had more activity in the brain region with the most dopamine receptors, the caudate nucleus. Those dogs also had less activity in the part of the brain associated with fear and anxiety, the amygdala.[19] These results are exciting, as they also point to our learning abilities as we share the same brain

---

[19] *Gregory Berns Knows What Your Dog Is Thinking (It's Sweet) - The New York Times (nytimes.com)*

structures. It also indicates that a confident dog will learn more successfully. Therefore, we must stay curious about our dogs and their breed and what, as an individual, they might need.

As for the barking and reactive dogs in training classes, be aware of their fear or arousal because of the movement of other dogs. My advice to these owners is to empathise with your dog's plight. The dog barking or a puppy frantically biting at its owner's hands will not be able to learn in a class. Perhaps ask your trainer for one-to-one lessons until your dog can cope. After you have honed your skills, I recommend desensitisation tactics. If your dog starts to bark in class and you are waiting your turn—keep them moving. Find yourself a space in the room and walk in circles, zigzag, or walk in a figure of eight. Make reassuring noises. Show them lots of encouragement.

The same goes for the puppy biting its owner—don't chastise your dog, but realise your dog is worried. Find a quiet corner of the class and just play with your dog. Remember, a dog that is stressed will not learn. So, it is pointless to carry out any exercises your instructor has given you. Instead, practise the activities in the home environment where your dog is relaxed. Then build up their confidence to take part in a class. Perhaps arrive to class early, and practise the exercises in the empty hall before anyone arrives. Then when everyone turns up, you could even practise some activities outside until your dog can cope. Do everything you can to build up your dog's confidence. Show them that life happens around them, and they need not worry.

The Gift of Curiosity

As human beings, we can be curious and learn about and experience new things. However, there are two types of curiosity for humans—the first is the curiosity for knowledge and the pleasure from investigating that knowledge. Then there is curiosity that comes from the lack of knowledge and the information gap, making us uncomfortable and restless, as we feel we need to know and find out about something. Just think about when a text arrived, and you were driving along and could not look. Did you stop to get your phone out?

When seeking information, we may sense an information gap, triggering uncomfortable feelings, notably if your dog exhibits undesired behaviours that you seem unable to stop. And in the dog training class, we will feel all the guilt and shame I described earlier. The feelings of guilt and shame may also arise when out and about. Perhaps your dog is under the table at a pub, and a strange dog walks in, which makes your dog kick-off. Suddenly, you feel that you are the worst dog owner ever. However, if you have no interest in the subject of dog training, you might be reluctant to push past that pain and prefer to stay shut down to new ideas. So, if we want to help our dogs, we must cultivate interest so that our minds thirst for knowledge.

Research by Tommy Blanchard et al. has shown that monkeys will give up the reward of a drink to find out more information.[20] So when we say we thirst for knowledge, it seems to be more than a metaphor. Therefore, we must stay in the Goldilock position between the pleasure of finding out and the uncertainty we feel when we experience the gap in our knowledge, which can provoke anxiety and stress. So as humans, we need to optimise curiosity-driven learning. However, it has been shown that those who suffer from excessive anxiety do not like to reach out for new experiences. New experiences bring up uncomfortable emotions, which evoke a fear response. When I ask clients to start to play with their dogs, they often become embarrassed. They do not like the feelings evoked by being asked to do something new. One client even described it to me as 'ritual humiliation.' Unfortunately, he did not understand the triggers of behaviour and reward at work in his brain. However, I believe if students were given an understanding of their emotional responses to learning, I think they would adopt a growth mindset.

Learning and emotional responses come from our primaeval brain; when we were Hunters-gatherers, we saw

---

[20] *Blanchard, Tommy C., Hayden, Benjamin Y., Bromberg-Martin, Ethan S. (February 4, 2015) Orbitofrontal Cortex Uses Distinct Codes for Different Choice Attributes in Decisions Motivated by Curiosity, Neuron 85 602–614 Cell Press*

food, ate the food, and felt good, which helped us to learn. When our ancestors ate the food, their brains gave them a dopamine hit (a feel-good chemical). Their brains said, *Remember this good feeling, this food, and where you found it.* Then evolution stepped in, and our evolving creative brains said, *Why don't you eat something to feel better when you feel mad or sad?* Sometimes, the signal to eat doesn't come from our stomachs but now comes from our brains. In turn, research has shown that we have a gut reaction to learning experiences. That is why we have a sinking feeling in our stomach when we have to do something new, like standing up and speaking in public or playing a game with our dog in front of other students. For some, the experience becomes so uncomfortable they will avoid the pain at all costs. Their whole body has hijacked them with fear.

However, we now understand how to overcome these fears. Even the most reluctant public speakers can learn to stand on stage in front of hundreds of people. Instead of fighting their reward-based learning process, they become curious about what made them uncomfortable.

You may be feeling uncomfortable right now. My advice is to stay with the feeling. Reach out for the biscuit tin if you need to, and mindfully take a bite; don't resist the urge or try and force yourself to learn what I am trying to outline for you. Instead, stay curious and become mindful of why you feel that way. Is it because you are stressed out, and all you want is answers to your dog's issues? Or is it because all this science stuff is reminding you of school? And you never liked school anyway. We either resonate with what we are learning, or we might experience resistance because of emotions that get stirred up within us. If our brains offer resistance, we will try and avoid the pain and will not be open to new ideas.

After years of teaching experience, when I come across clients whose brains have hijacked them, they usually say, "Yes, but I have done that, and it didn't help." They are just exhibiting avoidance, so I try not to react emotionally to their resistance. Still, I have to firmly point out that they must apply a can-do attitude when relating to their dog because a dog will mirror their human state of mind.

It might help to understand what is going on in our brains to help us cultivate curiosity-driven learning. As evolved humans, we need to understand the power of the prefrontal cortex, which will help you understand whether your reaction comes from interest or from the pain of not knowing. Our prefrontal cortex helps solve problems as we use the memory of that tasty food, and, as for primal man, we have learned where we can find it. The same applies when we seek out new information. When we are satisfied when we take in more knowledge, then the flavour is sweet. But if we seek information, and it does not satisfy, as when we find ourselves resistant to new ideas, that curiosity has a bitter flavour. We discover, therefore, that curiosity has two distinct flavours.

Consequently, when we feel dissatisfied with the information we have sought, we might feel the need to escape through other behaviours. That is why when we feel bad, we desire something sweet. Although our prefrontal cortex gives a cognitive understanding of our addictions, we seem unable to stop. For example, this earliest part of our evolved brain understands, from a rational viewpoint, that we should stop eating cookies to make ourselves feel good. Unfortunately, the brain's prefrontal cortex that controls this thinking stops working when we are stressed out. And the comfort eating habit continues as another part of the brain comes into play. Research shows that the roots of our cravings are centred in this part. The posterior cingulate cortex takes us on a ride of our desires; just one more biscuit, and I will feel better. However, this part of our brain quietens by becoming more mindful. Indeed, a food addict with an obesity problem can be asked to eat their favourite food mindfully. As they do so, they discover that the combination of fat, sugar, and salt is their addiction. They also learn their dislike of their overeating behaviour. However, solving the problem is not achieved by denying yourself, which is unsustainable. Instead, those consumed by their food addictions need a structured plan to overcome their overeating. They need to decide what they want.[21] Plus, it has been discovered if given a replacement behaviour, their weight drops without trying harder to diet.[22]

Similarly, we cannot force ourselves to stop or start feeling like we need to escape when faced with experiences that make us feel bad. Such a habit can only be broken by being curiously aware of what is happening within our brains. We must embrace our discomfort about finding new ways of doing things, including a paradigm shift in our understanding and learning about dogs' behaviour. Indeed, we can take note of our body sensations. We can become disenchanted on a gut level that we do not like our reactions to new ideas. When we understand that we are acting out of habit, we will likely make better choices. As in the case of controlling weight, the obese person can learn they do not, in reality, like their favourite biscuit. Rather, they see that their brain has been hijacked by the ratio of carbs to fat (roughly 1g fat to 2g carbs), which is a combination near to mother's milk. 'A 100ml serving of human breast milk contains around 4g fat and 8g carbs, making it surprisingly sweet.' Therefore, the first food we consumed as babies explains our addiction to this combination of fat to carbs. Food manufacturers have used this fact when

---

[21] *(507) David A. Kessler: The End of Overeating - Taking Control of the Insatiable American Appetite - YouTube*
[22] *A tip for those like me who want to stop eating biscuits. When you feel like eating just one more biscuit to feel better, go outside and play a game with your dog. They will thank you for it.*

processing biscuits etc., to profit from our cravings.[23] However, as consumers, the obese person can learn about this addiction. They can turn their curiosity into wisdom to help them succeed. Therefore, when we become mindful of our emotional responses, we can find the motivation and wisdom to try new approaches to our dog's struggles. Then, we are more likely to turn these struggles into pointers towards helping our dogs become all they can be. By staying curious, we will have the well-behaved dog we always wanted.

As Einstein put it, 'Curiosity has its own reason for existence. One cannot help but be in awe when he contemplates the mysteries of eternity, of life, of the marvellous structure of reality. It is enough if one tries merely to comprehend a little of this mystery each day. Never lose a holy curiosity.'[24]

So my advice is to become curious about your dog's behaviour and the new ideas in my book. You might feel cross with your dog, who has just stolen your sandwich. You might even feel cross at me, who tells you your dog is not being naughty and does not need punishment. And that I am telling you to try and understand why your dog did such a thing. As humans, we focus on the functional side of our relationship

---

[23] Mosley, Michael, Dr. the fast 800: How to combine rapid weight loss and intermittent fasting for long-term health, 2019 p.23
[24] https://www.psychologytoday.com/gb/blog/the-craving-mind/201909/curiosity-our-superpower-just-about-everything

with our dogs and try to think about how to stop them from doing the things we don't want them to do. I would humbly ask you to push past the pain of your resistance. Try and understand why your dog behaves as they do—a dog sees the kitchen counter as a generous benefactor. After all, it gave them a sandwich last time. The easiest way to teach a dog not to do that is to put the sandwich out of reach. That flavour of advice might be sweet to you. But what about if your dog is tall like my Leonberger? The advice is unsatisfactory—it has a bitter flavour. Then I must push past my resistance and think outside the box. How can I explain to my dog that she is only allowed food that I have given her permission to eat? I must resist the range of emotions I feel, from disappointment to downright anger. Yes, I still find my dogs can make me feel cross, but I have learned to understand myself and my emotional responses. I exchange anger for curiosity. From curiosity, I look to how I might take action. I play games that teach her that she can only have something on the cue 'get it.'

Dog training is a science that is continuously growing and evolving as we discover more about reinforcement training. I am thankful to the experts in the field of positive dog training. They have taught me so much about building a relationship with my dog. I am constantly learning and open to new ways of doing things. Today, I have moved away from concentrating on functional training. I am now thinking more about my dog's emotions. It has pushed me out of my comfort zone, and I have wanted to escape the discomfort, which is okay.

Games-based training will help both you and your dog. If you push past your discomfort, your dog will thank you for trying to understand its point of view. Our dogs are constantly curious and seeking information. Even the most fearful of dogs are alert to their environment. Though they may choose a coping behaviour we do not like, we can understand why they, too, may feel the need to escape. If we allow our dogs to think and choose the correct behaviour, we will gain far more success than training by the old ways of imposing our will on our dogs—a very human trait. Therefore, if we listen to our dogs and the games they like to play, I believe they can teach us how to be better humans and be open to new ideas and experiences. I think I am a better person because of it. Because of my dogs, I frequently discover more about myself. And I now look forward to where my dogs will lead me next.

PART II: WHAT IS A DOG?

We all have an idea about how our dog will fit into the family or how your dog will keep you company if you live alone. These ideas might originate from a memory of a sweet dog you owned as a child, and you want to recapture that for yourself or your children. It may even be your first dog. So, your idea of the relationship you are hoping for might come from stories you have read about or depictions of dogs you have seen on the screen. In my book, *In Search of Lassie*, I explored this idea, but suffice to say that the 'Lassie Myth' maintains the picture of the perfect dog.

It is not wrong to have high ideals and goals when we start on our journey of dog ownership. As C S Lewis so aptly puts it, 'Aim at heaven and you'll get earth "thrown in": aim at earth and you'll get neither.'[25] However, as we aim high, we need to understand what a dog is to unlock the roadblocks to achieving a good relationship with our dog. We must also appreciate how our poor reactions and emotions towards our dogs will damage our relationship with them. When we experience a conflict of feelings when our hopes are not met, we may be tempted to give up on our dog. We may even feel

---

[25] *Lewis, C S Mere Christianity. London: William Collins, 1952 p. 57*

resentful as we suffer from broken dreams. Then the dog is a constant reminder of this disappointment, which raises feelings of anger. This anger will mean our dogs will be less likely to want to be around us, and our dogs often mirror our moods and emotions with poor behaviour. As I explained in Part I, to achieve the relationship of our dreams, we need to be kinder to ourselves. If dogs mirror our state of mind, they will undoubtedly feel less stressed when we get in touch with our emotions, own up to them, and grow. As we become better humans, our dog is free to be their better selves.

We help our dogs reach their potential from the moment we bring them home. But don't think you have to do long sessions of training. I say to clients, "Every time you put the kettle on, play with your dog for five minutes and use a set of games that will give a sound basis for good manners around the house." Training and play should always come together. But never attempt to do either when you feel in a low mood, tired, or unwell. First, take care of your own needs to feel positive yourself. It is challenging to train your dog positively if you feel angry or upset. You may even be tempted to smack the dog on the nose for being naughty. Sadly, I have to ask owners not to punish their dogs physically. I also have to explain that shouting angrily at their dogs, or yanking on their lead, will negatively affect their relationship with the dog. As proven, a child should not be smacked or threatened at school, so we should not threaten or hit our dogs. Neither a child nor a dog will learn when there is a threat of punishment. Rather just play with your dog. That will restore you and your dog to a better frame of mind. Most training books focus on the functional side of dog training, how to get a dog to sit or come when called, etc. However, I want to reiterate that we must understand what a dog is. We also need to know how their emotions will affect us. As I watch dogs acting up in dog training classes, I see the interplay between the dog's frustrations and the feelings of its guardian. Much more emphasis should be given to this interplay between two sentient creatures with their own likes and dislikes. It is an important subject that deserves further investigation by every pet dog owner.

In this section of the book, I will discuss breed types. Of course, not all dogs fit into their breed type exactly, but the breed can be a good predictor of the behaviour you might expect. This section will explain how each dog is on a mission: to do the things that its breed type is wired to do. Some children are born artists, and others are innately athletic, so it is with our dogs. However, if you have a hunting breed currently living in your home and do not intend to take up a sporting life to fulfil your dog's hunting needs, do not despair. Try the games at the end of the book, scan the QR codes, and download dog training videos. Don't struggle until you have understood everything about what it is to be a dog, even though this will undoubtedly help in the long run to build a better relationship. Instead, go straight to the essential handy hints and start practising the games. You will be surprised just how quickly your relationship will begin to grow.

In my experience, when clients come to me, they need some quick fixes for managing their dog to keep harmony in the household. Clients particularly worry when their dog shows signs of aggression. However, reading your dog's body language and understanding the triggers of bad behaviour can prevent a dog from needing to resort to nipping. For example, I have had clients who have explained that their dog has snapped at their child because it was close to the dog's toy or bowl. If this is the case for you, I strongly suggest you employ a dog behaviourist. Do not hope for the best or start trawling the Internet for advice. There are so many different views in the public domain that may create even more problems with inappropriate advice for your situation. Each dog and each case is unique, so look for a qualified professional that will walk with you in helping to make the right decisions for you and your family.

If your dog is struggling, enrolling yourself into group dog training classes is equally not the way forward. It is better to go to a one-to-one lesson and build up your dog training skills and your dog's confidence before joining a group class.

Sadly, in my experience, more dog-to-dog aggression can occur when dogs go to dog training lessons for more than four weeks. For example, clients struggling with their dog's lunging and barking on a lead mistakenly bring them to classes to find that the experience escalates their dog's poor behaviour. They often believe the dog will get used to other dogs and that their dog will stop the behaviour with more socialisation. But instead, the dog just practises the behaviour because they have not been shown how to react differently. Dogs who carry out lunging and barking behaviour are then labelled as reactive. So I always strongly suggest that my clients enrol with me on a one-to-one basis so that I can give them the right tools to focus their dog even when other dogs are present. When the clients have been shown how to help the dog choose to walk nicely on their leash and have played boundary games, I believe they are more able to cope. Once clients have the skills to cope with exciting distractions, it is time to put these skills into practice with a group class or social walk. I prefer to give one-to-one lessons until I am sure the dog can cope with all environmental distractions and the owner understands what to do when these distractions cause their dog to react. These distractions might include the odd squirrel or jogger that might pass by, not to mention other dogs.

In this section, I will give advice about the general problems I encounter in my daily practice as a behaviourist and trainer that can be tackled by managing the dog's environment and game plans that can be applied throughout the day. Each training piece of advice will direct you to simple ways to overcome your struggles. However, remember your dog is an individual, and you might want to employ a professional to give you pointers. After all, we send our kids to school. Why should our dogs suffer from a lack of education from an expert? You might describe a dog as a toddler in fur. I am not saying children are like dogs. Still, there are a lot of comparisons you can make between the parenting of children and the raising of a well-adjusted dog. Indeed, I often refer to the owner as a guardian, as an owner should act as a parental leader. I believe you will see the benefits of such an approach and how it increases the successful relationship with your dog.

I have found that the old idea of enforcing your authority over the dog gains little long-term success. Instead, we need to consider the environment our dogs have been placed. We also need to understand the genetics underpinning their behaviour and how each dog is an individual with its very own character. By creating a culture of respect for the dog's needs, we will be on our way to building a better bond with our dog.

Chapter 4

DOG ON A MISSION

In this chapter, I let you into the secret sauce of dog training—your dog is learning 24/7. You may not think you are a dog trainer, but dogs learn from the environment every moment of the day. So, if you say you have not trained your dog, you are very much mistaken because everything you do throughout the day teaches your dog something. The secret sauce to dog training is to be intentional about what you teach. For example, we teach our dogs to jump up when we play with our puppies on the floor and think it is super cute when they lick at our faces. Our dogs get lots of information from our mouths, from our mood to what we ate the previous meal. When your dog becomes an adult, they still want to check on this information. So when problems arise and our dogs show poor choices, we need to make a paradigm shift.

Instead of thinking: *We have a 'bad dog,' and how can I stop the behaviour?,* we must think about how the behaviour started. Was it us or the environment that contributed to teaching the behaviour in the first place? Remember how puppies learned to jump up. Then we must think about how we can help our dogs make better choices rather than trying to stop the behaviour. For example, if you try to push your dog away when they are jumping over you and your guests. Your dog will instantly resist and even believe you want to play. As Pavlov discovered (a physiologist known for discovering classical conditioning), you are tapping into the opposition reflex (also known as the freedom reflex).[26] The opposition reflex is the resistance you get when you push or pull a dog. Your dog will automatically resist and push against your push or pull against your pull. So, when your dog jumps up when you return home, teach another behaviour incompatible with jumping up. An incompatible behaviour does not necessarily mean training your dog to perform a functional behaviour such as a sit or down.

A sit or a down-stay does not necessarily arrive at the calm behaviour you want. We have to think about the dog's emotional state at that moment. We have to think about their arousal level. Rather than think about functional behaviours,

---

[26] *Conditioned reflexes: An investigation of the physiological activity of the cerebral cortex - PMC (nih.gov)*

we need to help our dogs deal with their emotions rather than their behaviour. Only when we have taught them to self-regulate can we give them the attention they crave when the visitor arrives. We need our dogs to suppress their own excitable outbursts when visitors appear at the door. We need to teach them how to overcome their initial excitement so that they can modify their behaviour. For example, teach your dog to retrieve a favourite toy for you when you walk through the door, or you could throw food away from you for them to enjoy being scatter fed. Scatter feeding and retrieving a toy will dispel all their pent-up energy and calm your dog down. Then you will be able to have a calmer dog who can receive attention without jumping up frantically, which might end up in someone getting hurt.

Dogmanship

Dogmanship is a term I use to describe the guardian's ability to train and read their dog's behaviour and to adjust the dog's conduct to fit in with their lifestyle. In the past, we blamed the dog's behaviour on the dog's poor breeding or the owner's poor dogmanship. When I started my journey to good dogmanship, there was a fashion to say that the dog's future depended on the socialisation he had been given as a young puppy. But now we realise one form of dog training does not help every dog because it is a combination of nature and nurture, rather than one or the other. So gathering many puppies together without the proper supervision will not make a dog more friendly to other dogs in adult life. The opposite effect has proven to be the case. Unregulated puppy parties ended up in bullies learning to be better at fighting and shy dogs learning to fear other dogs. It is up to every guardian to learn how to acquire good dogmanship to lead their dog to become a good dog citizen. Every owner needs to invest in their dog's education to find the best solution for their dog, as every dog is an individual.

What Is a Dog?

The dog's personality is formed through its breeding, what job of work it was originally bred for, and the environment we have given the dog. Each dog will respond to its environment differently. Our mistake has been to lump together ideas of what a dog is. We often make a sweeping overview, which does not give enough credit for how a dog is an emotional, sentient creature. Like us, each dog has its own set of likes and dislikes making him unique, just as everyone on this planet is unique. They have personalities just as we do. So read on to find out what model of dog you have. What are its hardwired modes of behaviour?

Like a computer, a dog's genetics and the job it was designed to do will impact behaviour patterns. How it was raised as a puppy will also add to your dog's character. Thankfully, because of the research on the human brain, we have discovered how the dog's temperament can be moulded by playing games. Research has shown that the human brain can be rewired. We can change our hardwired reactions to specific triggers. For example, phobias can be overcome by cognitive behaviour therapy (CBT). So it is with our dogs. However, we cannot sit our dogs on a therapist's chair and talk through their phobias. But we can play games their breed loves in situations that might trigger a negative response. Suppose your small dog is fearful of large dogs. Playing games at a comfortable distance with your dog will help make your dog feel differently. Your dog will now see a large dog and think: *Great, I see a large dog, which means the games are about to start.* Thus proving, like humans, dogs have neuroplastic brains. The problems begin when we think we are stuck with our mental state and our dog's poor behaviour. Then the relationship between the dog and its guardian breaks down, and a vicious circle of negative interactions becomes ingrained. For example, a dog is trying to get to something in the environment it wants. When the dog becomes frustrated, it may start to bark. Then when it barks, the owner begins to restrain the dog, and the frustration leads to the dog's defiance (as seen in human terms). However, this is often not defiance but comes from the dog's need to escape, which builds up from its fear of losing out on what it desires. But if the owner does not recognise this, the pattern of conflict between owner and dog becomes ritualised. It is then advisable to have a trainer step in to break the cycle. The owner is unaware of the ritualised dance between them. The pattern can only be broken when the owner is shown how to satisfy the dog's needs in the environment where it has been placed.

A dog's reaction to its environment will differ for every dog, depending on the breeding. For example, in what choice the breeder made for mating, such as the temperament of the dog's mother. It has been shown that a nervous mother will produce fearful pups. When choosing a puppy, you ideally want to visit with the bitch first. Is she kind and biddable, or excitable and reactive? Although it is not always possible to meet the father, you can do due diligence and make sure the sire is equally a kind and biddable dog. There are so many different combinations, and not only are there these character traits, but the progeny of the mating will also inherit hardwired traits for behaviour accompanying breed type. Hunting dogs, Herding dogs, Guardian dogs, and Companion dogs will all give motor patterns that combine with how the puppy was raised. There is, however, a caveat to this selection process. Not all puppies have read the handbook for their breed. Indeed, my uncle had a German Shepherd far from his breed type—ironically, he was called Wolfy. But there was nothing scary about him; I remember him as a child as having the softest nature and certainly did not seem to have the guarding gene for which they are best known. I wonder if this was because he was a particularly fluffy German Shepherd.

Therefore, people saw him as a big teddy bear and reacted to him kindly.

Dogs are often perceived by their reputation. For example, in films, dogs such as the German Shepherd are used to guard or outrun the baddies and bring them down. Then the general population see a dog that looks very similar in shape and coat colour and will inadvertently step sideways when you walk down the street with them. My own Leonberger gets that reaction. And I know owners who express that same feeling when they walk the Rottweiller or Doberman. These two dog breeds are perceived as aggressive. But I wonder: What if we stepped away constantly from the floppy Labrador? Would we get a dog that becomes aggressive too? Probably. Are these guarding breeds then naturally aggressive? Yes! Can we breed aggression out of these breeds? Yes, but there are many confounding variables.

Much is being discussed in the dog world, human medicine, and psychology about epigenetics and how genes can become turned on by a single event. The programmed reactions are then passed down to future generations. Therefore, combinations of breed types, even in a mixed breed, will impact its temperament. And the environment it is brought up in will switch on these motor patterns to a lesser or greater extent. We only now understand how a human mother's temperament can impact her children's welfare. Mercifully, if this area in our lives was less than ideal, we are not stuck with the character our parents have passed on to us. We can learn to deal with our issues differently with a growth mindset. And so it is with our dogs. But if you are a first-time owner, it is better to know what you might have to take on with the dog you chose. For example, the hunting dog might not suit a family home. The motor patterns for a dog from the hunting dog group, orientation, eyestalk, chase, capture, bite, dissect, and eat, could be problematic. A sighthound might go through the whole pattern. The clash between its instincts and its guardian's expectations may lead to a breakdown of harmony within the household. Sadly, a family friend took her Yorkshire Terrier a walk with her daughter's greyhound, which ended badly. They were horrified. Indeed, anyone holding on to the perfect dog myth will be shocked by the animalistic side of their pet.

Dogs on a Mission and Family Therapy

We often buy a dog to cuddle up to as we sit on the sofa. We hope our dog will fill the need for connection in our lives, which is so woefully lacking in today's society. Then we are disappointed to find that the creature we have chosen to love reminds us of the imperfect world in which we live. We might have bought a puppy to make us feel better about life. For example, at the start of the pandemic in 2020, many people got a dog and households in the US acquired almost nine million—equivalent to the population of New York City.[27] Thus proving the work of the modern dog is to fill the gap of emotional support in our fractured and disconnected world. However, the therapeutic benefits of a dog cannot be experienced when the dog is managed incorrectly. The journey of dog ownership can be a stony path without the correct understanding of what a dog is. My friend's daughter, whose greyhound chased and killed their mother's Yorkshire Terrier, did not understand their dog and blamed the dog for his behaviour. However, he was only acting on his instinct. After all, he was hardwired to run after small furry creatures. Man has even created a sport around the sighthound's desire to hunt and chase. Indeed, many of our breeds originated with a job of work in mind. The confinement within the urban home was never in the minds of the original designers of breed types. Except for Companion dog breeds, most dogs were bred to be active throughout the day. Still, even the lap dog has genetic roots within a working stock. For example, the Bishon Frise have a poodle-type background. With their clever and jolly dispositions, it is clear that being ignored most of the day is detrimental to their welfare.

Sadly, we sometimes confine our dogs for over eight hours in a house with nothing to do. It is like asking a toddler to sit down and stay focused on the blackboard whilst the teacher

---

[27] Chalabi, Mona, (2022, January 22) *Pets prove to be the pandemic's cute, furry growth area. Pets prove to be the pandemic's cute, furry growth area | Pets | The Guardian*

describes Newton's Laws of Motion. We can predict this to be an unsuccessful venture. And so, trying to have a working dog confined to the urban home will also cause the opposite and equal reaction. As we apply the pressure of confinement, equal suppressed energy will be ready to explode at any moment. Even though we desire to own a calm dog, our dog will show their need to meet its breed needs and fulfil them, and our dogs will engage in unwanted behaviours. A terrier, for example, who desires to hunt out rats may become vigilant to noises around your house and start digging at your walls.

Like many before, new owners have discovered that their dog is not suited for their lifestyle. These new guardians of their pet dog underestimated the commitment needed. I hope this book will address the needs of both a new dog owner and the dog's welfare and prevent the high number of dogs from being relinquished to rehoming centres.

My greatest desire is to see safe ownership of dogs. For example, it is vital to create well-adjusted dogs who can fit into the family home and the community in which that home exists. Dog ownership has exploded in urban environments causing far more ambivalent exchanges with other dogs and people living alongside us. However, the more worrying cases of dog bites come from incidents between owners and their own family dogs. Therefore, I would encourage any potential dog owner to think carefully about the breed of dog they might bring into their home. Many clients ask me what breed might be more suitable. The answer to this question is not as simple as it may seem. It may be suggested that anyone seeking an emotional support dog should choose a 'Toy Breed' (a category of Companion dogs identified by the Kennel Club). However, ironically the dog most likely to bite its owners comes from this category. Therefore, you might be tempted to look at the giant breed known for its gentleness. Although they may be known as gentle giants, these dogs can also bite; but their bites can go through a bone. Therefore, no one can be complacent; all dogs can bite. But a dog will only bite if put in a situation that triggers fear or extreme frustration because of its breed needs and the miscommunication and poor handling between owner and dog.

However, my greatest desire is for you, dear reader, to have the information to prevent the situation that escalates to your dog biting someone in the family. So if you have already realised you have a dog from a working background with lots of surplus energy or a nervous dog scared of his own shadow, then you may think you have made an awful mistake in getting the dog in the first place, especially if your dog has snapped at you or your children. However, do not despair; there is a way through this miscommunication. I advise reaching out and getting help from a behaviourist and trainer and researching your dog's breed type and possible motor patterns that will go with that breed type. There may have been a logical reason in the dog's mind why they did such a thing.

For example, you may have tried to take something from them, like a stolen sock or shoe. Indeed, rather than functionally training your dog to relinquish an article, think about why it took it in the first place. Everyone who owns a dog must become their own dog's ethologist, for no one knows your dog better.

The hunting dog bred to retrieve who snaps at you may suffer from resource guarding tendencies. Guarding an acquired item does not show that the dog is misbehaving. When it snaps at someone trying to remove a stolen item, it is just acting on its hardwiring. The dog is only trying to carry out its job. We wanted dogs to hold things in its mouth and not let them go, and then we, as pet dog owners, rush around madly trying to grab the stolen item from them. As the more clever of the two species, we must recognise how we can transfer the value of keeping something in the mouth to relinquishing the item on cue. I say on cue because we run into problems when we think a dog should act on our commands, and if they do not, the dog must suffer the consequences.

Clients' emotions are often heightened when they approach me for help with resource guarding issues. They believe their dog has turned 'bad' and needs to be rehomed because it is not doing what they say. They believe the dog has a dominant temperament and must be shown who is in charge. Therefore they want me to show them how to administer consequences to get the dog to do what they command. As a human race, we still do not understand how to be kind to the animals in our care, let alone be kind to our fellow human beings. A dog with resource guarding issues needs understanding, not punishment. Instead of punishing our dogs, we can teach our dogs how to bring back items to us. And when they have something we don't want them to have, we need to teach them how to swap the item for something else.[28] But always remember, anything taken to the dog's bed or taken to a hiding place must not be challenged by the owner, especially by the children of the family. I like to keep puppies on training leads so they cannot take stolen items to a hiding place. If you are stuck in a cycle of resource guarding, seek a behaviourist's help. But, as a rule of thumb, if you have a gun dog, you must be aware as a whole family what might trigger resource guarding and the possibility of getting bitten.

Every owner needs to sit down and discuss with the family how together they might fulfil their dog's breed needs and delegate responsibility to each family member. As everyone in the family becomes invested in the dog's progress, you will be amazed at how this will change your dog's outlook on life. Indeed, talking together about feelings and frustrations will positively impact family relationships whilst creating a plan to help your dog cope with busy family life.

---

[28] *See Swapsies Games at the back of the book*

Chapter 5

OUT AND ABOUT

Our dogs need understanding and support to fit in with the busy urban environments they find themselves in today. In the past, fewer clashes occurred between other dogs and people, as our dogs would take themselves off on walks. But, in recent history, we have not allowed the free reign of dogs on our streets. I am not advocating this as a solution (there are far too many dogs today). Still, I would promote training dealing with your dog's pent-up energy levels. Just think about taking your child on a long-haul flight. Remember how they screamed and became grouchy when they were on the plane? Remember how they ran ahead in absolute abandon when you finally got to your destination—glad to be free of the plane's confinement. Think about how much pent-up energy our dogs have as they are confined to the house most of the day. We need to give our dogs outlets for their energy. Unfortunately, some owners believe this is achieved by taking the dogs on two daily walks. On one level, two walks may seem to be the solution, but on another, it can be a disaster. If your dog misbehaves, two walks a day will only now achieve a fit naughty dog.

The solution to your dog's pent-up energy is to schedule game-based training throughout the day. Daily games utilise not only their pent-up physical energy but also help their frustration. You can give them a game to play every time you put the kettle on. Or allow your dog to assume the task of being your companion as you carry out necessary chores. Something my dog is doing right now as my husband mows the lawn; Joy has taken her usual place where she considers herself to be on duty. Sitting on duty fulfils Joy's desire to guard; a Leonberger is a breed categorised as a Guardian breed. She knows that her owner will not be aware of any approaches above the noise of the lawnmower. However, I have also taught Joy that she must cease on cue once she has alerted us to possible threats. I thank her for doing a great job by telling her calmly, "Thank you, that will do." I then ask her to pop up on her bed, which is incompatible with her usual desire to run up and down the fence to send away any intruders.

Here I must make a caveat. You can only allow your dog the privilege of guard duty if you are sure your dog is under your control. You cannot allow an untrained dog who will go into the red zone to have this privilege. Your dog must be trained to return when called, no matter the distraction. And even with a trained dog, you must take care of the arousal levels. Suppose you notice your dog goes into high arousal, i.e. unable to hear you. Then, you must go back to training an instant recall away from distractions. Plus, you must ensure your dog is not allowed free access to the area where you know your dog will be on guard duty. For Joy, this is sitting on the front doorstep.

If you have a giant Guardian breed, you must be extremely careful with its training. Hence, you never put them in a position where they think they should bite someone who comes onto your property. I practise sending Joy to a raised platform in the garden every day, and she will practise that behaviour throughout her life. The platform indicates a boundary she must not get off until I give her the release cue, 'free.' I call this game 'joyful stays,' as it allows me to carry out chores around the garden and fulfils Joy's breed needs.

'Joyful stays' is a great game. I play the game; stay on your boundary on another bed in the house. Then I leave the room to perform a chore out of sight. By teaching Joy to stay within her boundary when I am not present, I am teaching my dog to be more confident, which is essential when going out and about. I also ensure that Joy does not always follow me, as this activity can create separation anxiety if left unchecked.

It is out and about when an owner usually discovers the real character of their dog. The dog's character and personality typically appear between fourteen–sixteen weeks of age when the innate instincts of a dog's breed kick into place. It is when dogs have lost their puppyhood and are burgeoning adolescents. During adolescents, owners are often shocked by their dog's behaviour. For example, a client told me how horrified she was that her friendly and biddable Golden Retriever had chased down a deer and killed it. I, too, have been horrified by the animalistic side of my Leonberger. She managed to capture a pheasant and kill and dissect it before I got to her. So many owners have told me this same story. Thankfully, such scenarios need not be repeated with the correct management and training games.

The Plight of a Working Dog

My own experience of owning a working dog has opened my eyes to the plight of many a pet dog. My two Border Collies have pushed me to be inventive in my training to replace their need to work. I have two Border Collies who I have had to be inventive in my training to replace their need to work. I have had to become their sheep by engaging them in such activities as heelwork to music. I have known only too well the consequences of ignoring their hardwiring. The first problem I encountered was with my oldest collie, Fred. He taught me much about owning a working dog to whom this book is dedicated. It was a lovely sunny morning, and I set off for a walk in a local thicket at the edge of a meadow. He was just a puppy, and I lifted him from the boot of my car and set off, ready to play some hide-and-seek games to train him to come back when he was called. I had done all the right things with Fred. I had taught him first to find me when I hid behind a sofa or when I hid in another room—a great game to play for a puppy. I often tell my clients, "If your dog does not come when called when you are in the house, they will not come back when out for a walk." As I played hide and seek games in a local thicket at the edge of a meadow, I realised Fred had gone feral.

I was hiding behind a tree, waiting for a giddy puppy to race and enthusiastically greet me, saying, "You can't fool me." Then I heard giggles. I stopped hiding and stepped into a clearing to find a group of primary school children huddled together as my puppy was racing excitedly in circles around them. I called him from his self-made game, put him on the lead, and apologised to the teacher. Laughing, she thanked me for rounding up her children. That was a happy end to a story, but I realised that the children might not be giggling if Fred had been a fully grown dog when he might have been more intimidating. He might have, as an adult, nipped at the heels of a reluctant child.

Nipping is a tactic that many a Border Collie has employed to move a reluctant sheep or cow that has decided to stand its ground. Not something that shepherds like to have passed on to progeny when breeding a working sheepdog, as they do not want bruised lambs going off to market. However, the occasional nipping collie does slip through the net—probably because some Border Collies are used to round up cattle. The nip would not have been a problem for the cattle farmer. A Border Collie with all its working traits needs daily management in a pet home, for when children run, a collie is inclined to nip at heels just for fun. Indeed, one client pointed out that she decided not to buy a collie because they were such high maintenance. She is right.

Using Your Dog's Opus

The working Border Collie is on a mission. They see something moving, and they are hardwired to give chase. They become stir-crazy when they are not allowed to carry out their breed need to herd. Even as an older dog, my collie Fred still wants to work. So, when owners ask me, "When will my dog calm down?" I must answer if it is from working stock, probably never. However, you can use their enthusiasm for life for a particular job. Giving your dog a job also helps manage your dog's enthusiasm for carrying out the hardwired motor pattern of his breed. That is why I love to work for the dog charity Dog A.I.D. Clients are training their pet dogs to assist them in everyday tasks—from picking up a dropped pen to loading the washing machine. They use the dog's opus for daily functions by tapping into its innate instincts. For example, a gun dog breed loves to hold things in its mouth and retrieve items. The enthusiast of this breed constantly selected dogs who strongly showed this motor pattern. So, a new owner of a gun dog breed cannot get away from their dog's strong desire to carry out its opus. Like humans, this dog was born to carry out a task in life. Unlike humans, it knows what that task is. The problems start when we don't allow our dog to express their breed's opus.

Humans should utilise their dog's opus to create harmony in the household. However, clients needing a dog assistant must also be realistic about their dog's abilities and whether their breed matches their needs. For example, a dog supporting someone with physical conditions, such as a steadying role for a vertigo sufferer, must be the right height and strength to do that job. And for mobility issues, it is not fair to expect a small dog to pick up and carry a heavy object like a walking stick.

Breed Needs

After studying dog behaviour for many years and working with countless family pets, I have realised that every dog has its own needs. Like people, each dog is an individual with a particular temperament. Its breed may not always indicate its behaviour. The breed can give a hint of what you might expect. However, how much time we spend with our pets predicts the outcome.

By providing our dogs with the opportunity to socialise and play training games, we are more likely to build resilient dogs able to cope with our busy urban lives. We will succeed in creating a biddable character, happy to go along with what we want. We will give our dogs the tools to understand how to choose the correct behaviour in different scenarios. We will have a dog we will be proud to take out and about.

However, don't forget that dogs of all breeds might show normal behaviour that we might not want. For example, a toy breed might show guarding. But the toy breed would be of little use to the police force as my uncle's dog—Wolfy showed no guarding skills. Like Wolfy, a German Shepherd, dogs do not come out of the womb, having read the short descriptions often given for their breed type. Indeed, we must be prepared to see all of the traits of a dog in all of our breeds, from biddable behaviours often associated with the toy breed to the other end of the spectrum of fierce and defensive guarders often related to the large herding dogs. Am I contradicting myself? No, I am confident that a purebred dog, instead of the 'Mutt,' will show traits, coat colour, stature, and conformation. And there is evidence for a link between confirmation and possible temperament traits. For example, the Dachshund with the genetic mutation of short legs may show increased fear and aggression. The genes for both share the same chromosome[29]. Plus, the purebred dog will hint at its behavioural patterns, even if digging, hunting, herding, guarding, or any other attribute might appear in any dog. Other characteristics, such as temperament, can be predicted by a combination of nurture and nature, not one or the other. So, as with our children, we will never know if our dogs will fully reach their full potential unless we put the work into their education. However, my mission is to make that work into a game rather than a chore. Otherwise, how else are dogs going to survive in their environment?

Our homes are a dog's natural environment. Many cannot survive the street or kennel life that other feral dogs can survive. Indeed, sadly many street dogs are rescued with the misguided belief of giving them a better existence. I have found that many of these dogs find being brought in from abroad traumatic. Being kept in the confinement of a kennel or an urban home was beyond their capabilities. It is then that a true culture clash arises between human and dog when the dog shows its teeth and refuses to be stroked. These dogs need the input of an individual with heightened dogmanship. And even then, I would think twice as to whether we are genuinely

---

[29] *Zapata, Isain, James A Serpell, and Carlos E Alvarez. "Genetic Mapping of Canine Fear and Aggression." BMC genomics, August 8, 2016. https://www.ncbi.nlm.nih.gov/pmc/articles/PMC4977763/.*

saving these feral dogs who have been born to take care of themselves in the wild of the garbage dump. However, there are exceptions; these are the dogs that have joined the feral pack after being abandoned. Therefore, rehabilitation is more likely to be successful.

When choosing our dog, we need to understand its breed needs and background to give them suitable games to satisfy their breed needs. With help, their breed and its characteristics can be accommodated with our attention and games. We cannot make sweeping statements about what breed type would have the best temperament to cope with our busy urban environment. For example, saying that all Labradors are even-tempered is misleading to the new dog owner. There will always be a dog far from that breed description. It is better when choosing a puppy to look at the parents' temperament rather than choosing entirely by the short breed descriptions often given on the Internet. For example, it has been shown that all dog breeds have distinct nervous strains. Indeed, two recognised breeds, the Pointer and the Labrador have been identified as suffering from a particularly severe nervous strain. In my experience, I have seen very nervous Labradoodles, Shelties, and many more. A nervous strain is much more likely to cause problems in adulthood. For example, the puppy who is not bouncing around and playing in socialisation class has a proud owner who thinks how well-behaved their puppy is. But the puppy is likely to be nervous.

If this is not addressed, it can result in the puppy adopting one of the five F's as a strategy to cope with their fear. The worst of these is: fight.

As a dog lover, I question what has changed in our communities, causing the increase in fatal dog bites. I do not believe that the banning of breed types is the solution. It gives us a false sense of security in that it is all about breeding and not about our own behaviour, which might be causing the rise in dog aggression. Dogs have no other place to call home since canine familiaris adapted to live alongside us. We adopted their skills for our purposes. Therefore, we must take responsibility for the rise in problem dogs. For example, efforts to counteract the breeding of dogs in large numbers on puppy farms must be stopped, together with the plight of dogs bred and trained to fight.

Sadly, there is not only the carrying of knives for use as a possible weapon, but there is now a rise in dogs as a weapon. Gangs use many old fighting breeds as status symbols. Still, many do not have the skills to train them satisfactorily. Recently, it has been children who have become a victim of these status dogs rather than the intended rival gang. Now, we need to bring education to both people and their dogs to help them live in harmony with their communities. Education within our urban communities might be the answer, rather than banning certain types of dogs. Education within schools and prisons might be introduced to help those known to like these dogs for their look and status. They could be given training in kind and effective handling and care for these dogs. Instead, these old fighting breeds, used for bull baiting during Victorian times, could be given new activities to show their dog's prowess—such as pulling weights. I believe it would not only help the dog, but it even might help the human being to change their behaviour.

However, I digress, as I am sure you are not someone who intends their dog to attack a person or another dog. Although, I would caution you if you have adopted a dog that might have origins from one of the old Victorian fighting breeds from a rescue centre. These dogs can make lovely pets if given the proper outlet. However, you may need to assess your new dog's ability to cope with other humans and dogs. I have come across owners who have found out that their new rescue dog has little in the way of social skills. With the correct training, it may well be rehabilitated. Still, it would take all your energy and time. You would have to teach the dog how to grab toys for its fighting outlet and give up that toy on cue. You would have to create games for the dog to come away from other dogs and give it plenty of rewards when it was able to ignore other dogs. But still, even then, a dog with a bite history cannot be fully trusted. It would be better not to put them in a situation where they felt the need to fight. Regrettably, some of these dogs were punished by their original owners for disengaging from battle.

Unfortunately, those owning dogs from the original fighting breeds get poor reactions from other dog owners when out and about, probably because of everyone's natural fear of these breeds. But, in my experience, many of these dogs have great big hearts and are lovely with other people and dogs if bred and treated correctly. All the same, I would give all dogs their space and walk an arch around another dog if I had my dog on a lead—the natural and polite way a dog would approach another dog if it were free to do so.

Understanding how to interact with other dogs when your dog is on a lead is essential. Social training classes are so beneficial for helping dogs understand how to be around other dogs both on and off a lead. But choose your classes carefully. Some dogs will find such a class too challenging, leading to problematic behaviour. For example, for the owner with a nervous and reactive dog, I strongly suggest you get your mechanics right before taking them into a class. These anxious dogs still need guidance regarding appropriate behaviours, but this can be done in the comfort of your home. You can then learn how you might approach scenarios more successfully by building up your dog's confidence and working on your leash mechanics.

Sadly, I still see lots of yanking and popping of leads when a dog misbehaves in class. Such behaviour is not the owner's fault because the news of kind and effective training has still not filtered into the general public's understanding. As dogs are on a mission to fulfil their breed needs, the training class is where there is a clash of cultures. The clash of cultures occurs when the dog's desire to chase the little Dachshund on the other side of the room clashes with the owner's desire to have a well-behaved dog trotting beside them without yet understanding the mechanics of loose leash walking. I believe my game plans are the solution.

Chapter 6

GAME PLANS

Dogs love games. Research has shown that dogs prefer to work for their food rather than have food readily available in a bowl—termed Contrafreeloading. This fact can be seen in Ray Coppinger's research of Mexican free-ranging dogs. The origin of the domesticated dog, Ray Coppinger believed, came from the niche created by man. When humankind first settled in villages, dogs found their refuse dump as a source of available food. Villagers adopted the more friendly dogs. Coppinger's hypothesis is interesting, and indeed, research has shown that our dogs enjoy hunting out for their food. When the dog is denied this opportunity, it often shows signs of anxiety and depression. They can also be over-reactive in specific scenarios. Research has shown an improvement in animals' mental state if allowed to carry out natural behaviours such as seeking out their daily rations.

Ray Coppinger's research on free-ranging dogs has gone a long way to help us understand why a culture clash exists between dogs and men in the West.[30] Much of the free-ranging dogs' hedonic budget is fulfilled by searching for their food.[31] Therefore, these free-ranging dogs do not show the problems we experience. For example, reactivity is often demonstrated in the working dog when kept in the confinement of an urban home. I often describe this phenomenon as cabin fever in dogs. Over recent years, we probably all know how the dog feels. We have all been penned up in our houses for fear of catching or spreading Covid. However, there has been a relaxation in legislation, and everyone is desperate to return to normality. Unfortunately, our infrastructure cannot cope with the increased needs of its people to travel. There has been a lot of frustration shown in airports at the very moment I am writing this. Some people have found it difficult to contain their anger, and I believe if they were a German Shepherd, they would probably bite someone. So, if this is true for people, let us be more sympathetic towards the dog confined to the modern urban environment. Today the free-ranging dog is no longer tolerated. When I was a child, it was not unusual to have dogs who were allowed to take themselves out for a walk for their

---

[30] Coppinger, Raymond; Freinstein, Mark **How Dogs Work** Chicago, The University of Chicago Press, 2015
[31] Hedonic budget is a term used by COAPE to describe the breed activities needed to fulfil the dog's needs to stay in a healthy mental state.

amusement. It is only recently that society has not accepted it as the norm. Also, with the rise of dog numbers, it would be impractical.

Brain Games

First of all, no one works without wages. It is the same for a dog. My dogs work for part of their food ration. That does not mean you keep your dog hungry to control them. Indeed, that will cause more problems, such as resource guarding. However, we need to keep an eye on the amount of food our dog eats throughout the day so that they do not become overweight. Training should consist of tapping into our dog's need to work for their ration. We tap into their desire to gain food through Contrafreeloading. My dogs love to follow me when out on a walk as they are ready to earn their favourite treat. I feel so sad for those dogs whose owners insist their dogs should come back when they don't even give them any motivation to do so. Here, I know there is criticism of always relying on food to reward wanted behaviour. However, as I explained earlier, praise can be of equal benefit. But to get to that point, we must shape the desired behaviour. Then, once our dog carries out a good recall, we must continually praise when our dogs get the behaviour right. So often, as humans, we tend to focus on poor behaviour instead of remembering to praise the good things our dogs do.

Contrafreeloading behaviour, which means when offered a choice, a dog prefers to work for their food rather than accept food in a bowl, can be utilised to focus a dog's attention. The trick for an owner is to create enjoyment around working for their food. By introducing working for their food-ration, behaviour issues often diminish.

However, clients often tell me that their dogs do not accept food or even want to play with toys as a reward, and they find it difficult to motivate their dogs. For this reason, Guide Dogs for the Blind have taken to breeding dogs happy to work for treats. But that has caused its own problems as handlers have found that these dogs also have a propensity to put on too much weight. Therefore, it is essential to watch your dog's body condition and provide appropriate rations to the dog's condition, rather than just feeding the quantities suggested on your dog's diet packet.

If you have a dog that likes its food, you are fortunate, and playing my game plans will come easy to you and your dog. But if your dog is nervous and does not like food or toys, you will have to teach them how to approach life positively and that interactions with you are something to be sought out. To build fun interactions with your dog, you must discover your dog's favourite thing to do and then transfer the value of that activity to food or a toy for training. With my dog Fred, I found he loved to chase bubbles. So, I transferred the fun of chasing bubbles to his training regime. Although he preferred bubbles to treats and toys, he accepted a treat, knowing the bubbles came next. I then dropped playing bubbles every time.

If your dog does not play, I believe it may indicate that it is anxious or depressed. To overcome a dog's negative emotions, we must show them the joy of play and discover our own sense of fun along the way. I can say this with absolute assurance because my Leonberger neither liked food nor games. I had to teach her to enjoy both by incorporating her favourite things, just as I did with Fred. She loves the hose pipe, although I am now transferring that value to bubbles since the hose pipe ban came into force in our area.

I have owned dogs for many years, and each new dog teaches me a new lesson about dog ownership. Fred taught me how to play with an enthusiastic and highly driven dog, and Joy is right on the other end of the spectrum. However, both dogs have a brain and have benefited from my brain-stimulating games.

Training versus Play

Playing with the dog can often override a dog's need to take notice of its usual triggers to make a fear response. As a fully qualified dog behaviourist and trainer, I have helped many dogs and their owners in all walks of life. I have helped train dogs for sports and a specific job in the service dog community. And for every client, there an issue to overcome. For some, the dog desires to hunt; for others, it is a dog that is nervous and scared of people, other dogs, or both. These issues are on a sliding scale—from very withdrawn and anxious to extremely excitable and outgoing. However, by focusing on functional training, these problems persist. Instead, an owner needs to create a new story to move forward. I often ask the owner to leave behind the story that has been rehearsed in the past and ask them to tell me a new story, as if they are fast-forwarding into the future and I have waved a magic wand over their dog to make it be just as they had hoped. I suggest they write the story down on physical paper—there is something very positive about using pencil and paper. It could be written like a good newspaper article that we love reading. You might think this is pie-in-the-sky thinking, but I believe you will see how it is a reachable goal if you work backwards from the final story.

Why not try writing your dog's story? It has been proven that you are more likely to achieve goals if you have the end plan in sight. Goals can then be broken down. First, make a six-year plan describing the goals you want to meet. Then make a three-year plan, a one-year plan, a weekly plan, and then finally, a daily schedule. Making goals is especially relevant to those training dogs to be service dogs. They have goals to meet within the first three years of a dog's life. They must be focused and not allow the dog's education to drift.

Please refer to the epilogue, where I endeavour to pass on the primary games to underpin your dog's education. Often I am asked: "What advice would you give to a new dog owner?" I would have to reply: "Know yourself, and know your dog."

There is a mental impact of bringing another sentient creature into the household. When we understand our motivations, we can overcome our roadblocks to achieving the goals we are looking for in our dogs. We can see that training sessions have become play by writing down goals and adopting the goal-plan games. The chore of training is then taken away from our dog-owning equation. We can relax knowing that each coffee break becomes a play session. And each play session moves us closer to reaching the relationship with our dogs we always wanted.

Feelings of inadequacy because of our dog's poor behaviour are often something that many new dog owners would like to brush over or even deny. Undoubtedly, our mental state will affect our dogs and vice versa. But, be assured that dog behaviourists, like me, have gone through the same feelings; if they have not, walk away. Look for someone who will be able to come alongside you on a collaborative journey leading to doggy enlightenment. But until you find the right person, I hope this book will help you find the joy of owning a dog.

Rediscover Joy with Your Dog

Joy is elusive in this world that predominantly runs on anxiety—you just have to watch the news and feel the overall atmosphere that the world is living in today. How information is now related to us has changed over the last twenty years. We can no longer avoid it, and news programmes use emotive sound bites to hook us into 24/7 viewing. So it is not surprising that negative news impacts our anxiety levels—sadly for some, causing depression and mental health issues. There is a constant flow of news about climate change and pandemics, so it is not surprising that dogs have taken the new role of emotional support.

The idea of a dog fulfilling our needs is now being underpinned by research. However, research shows that our assistant dogs are under undue pressure because of the responsibility we put on them. Our support dogs are now needing to be supported themselves. It has come to light that some guide dogs develop behaviour problems during their training, resulting in lower chances of becoming fully-fledged guide dogs. The dogs' welfare is impacted as they are returned to the training centre. Studies have shown that the bonding with the guide dog's eventual owner is affected. Although they showed behavioural restraint, they had higher cardiac activation when separated from their owner.[32] Bremhorst et al.'s research has also highlighted how we might bring back joy to our everyday ownership. When we start looking at the

---

[32] Bremhorst, Annika, et al. Animals: an Open Access Journal from MDPI Animals | Free Full-Text | Spotlight on Assistance Dogs—Legislation, Welfare and Research | HTML (mdpi.com).

welfare of the dog, rather than just seeing the dog as a tool for our own use, there is a shift in thinking. As we start thinking about the dog's welfare, we can understand how we need to invest in our mental health. We can come together as a team, where it isn't all about us, and it isn't all about our dogs. It is not either or; it is about both. By understanding this, we can fill our emotional energy tank with the joy we need to help our dogs find their joy in life. By focusing on how to fulfil your dog's breed needs and looking to your own needs, we can build a strong bond that improves your dog's mood and mental health as well as your own. On the way, you will rediscover life in all its fulness, where you and your dog can live in harmony. Perhaps, you might even see life from a child's viewpoint.

A child can teach us much about what we have lost as adults. For example, the gift of curiosity has not been lost by a child who is constantly asking why. I would also say that life's joy can often be seen in a young child being taught something new. My granddaughter jiggles about with excitement when I say, "Shall I show you how it works?" I might be explaining something that to an adult might be seen as mundane and of little interest. For example, the other day, I explained how to open the peddle bin so she could throw away her sweet wrapper. After trying for herself, she jumped up and down shouting, "I did it," with absolute glee and excitement. That is indeed the joy we need to recapture within our mindset.

We can only help dogs once we rediscover joy. Again we need to find outlets for them to find the joy of living, from searching out new and exciting scents on a walk to the thrill of the chase created by the 'Whip It game' found at the end of my book. I suggest owners play games with their dogs throughout the day. Then as you play games with your dog, you will develop a sense of excitement that will uplift you. And as emotions have energy, you will understand how joy positively motivates you and even increases your energy levels throughout the day. However, for the dear reader who finds it embarrassing when trying out new things or says, "This kind of thing isn't for me." Try my game plan worksheets, expand your story, and give it a new ending. Find someone who has gone before you on the journey of doggy enlightenment and see how they are living their joy. When you have achieved the relationship you always wanted, you can be a role model for someone else by living a new joyful life with your dog. Nothing is more significant than someone commenting on your dog's fantastic behaviour and then asking how you got your dog to do that. At that point, my joy steps in, and as I grin from ear to ear, I say: "I play and have fun with my dog. It's that simple."

Dogs love to have fun, too, and much like children, they love to discover new things and play new games. Just ask my old dog Fred to who this book is dedicated. Now Fred is an old dog with arthritis. In the morning, walking around the garden, he follows close by my side. Then Fred sees the pop-up bed, where he knows games will start and jumps on the platform. He looks at me with expectation. And so, his daily routine of training begins. What game shall we play, he seems to ask. Show me something new—shall I run out to a pole, wrap around the pole and back to the platform? Can I go on a search game for a ball thrown into the long grass? His list of fun and the words he understands is endless. I was once asked by a dear friend looking after Fred for a week for a list of his cues as he wanted to get them right whilst I was away. I handed him a complete foolscap list of cues because Fred was training for a heelwork to music routine at the time. Tony laughed as he took the sheet of cues, but I think my friend had lots of fun, as well as Fred.[33]

---

[33] *Sadly, whilst writing this book my friend Tony Johnson of Africandawn Kennels passed away. Although this book is dedicated to Fred, I cannot neglect to express my thanks to Tony for all his help and support to my husband and I over the years during our journey towards doggy enlightenment. Tony will be sadly missed by all those who knew and loved him.*

EPILOGUE

Now you have read the book, or you may have even taken my advice and headed straight to the back to find out the games I have suggested. Whatever the case—welcome to a new way of being with your dog. Through the following few pages, you will find true harmony again in your household by carrying out the games-based training plan.

The Joy of Dog Game-Plan Vision Worksheets

The reason I created games-based training plans was really for myself. Like many dog owners, I dreamed of doing great things when I bought my new puppy. However, the road to doggy enlightenment can have its thistles and thorns along the way, and we all can suffer from broken expectations. By making plans, I felt empowered by the activity, which gave traction to my ideas. I can set down on paper what the relationship with Joy could look like as I projected my vision into the future. For it has been said in my favourite book that a man without a vision shall perish.

The benefit of writing down your story is not a new idea. As an English Scholar, I realise the importance of stories and how writing a projected narrative can give light to the next steps I need to make for them to come about.

Today, we understand how we learn through stories— from childhood to adulthood. Indeed, the use of narrative therapy has been used for years. Stepping away from the anxieties created by any relationship using narrative planning can help us see how we can develop greater self-compassion. As I say in my book, *In Search of Lassie: A Dog Owner's Guide to the Lassie Myth,* stories help us realise that we are not alone. So I have adapted the ideas from renowned enthusiasts of these concepts. First, as prescribed, I saw myself separate from the problems I experienced and then went on to write a preferred storyline for my dog, Joy. Having this storyline in front of me allows me to set goals and see training issues objectively to find solutions. Plans help me to see what I need to do to meet my story of the projected future for Joy. By writing a new storyline for Joy, I see how I have more agency than I first believed. I can make positive changes in her life and become the hero in her story.

Now our dogs are hardwired to become Herders, Hunters, Guardian, or Companion dogs. We are equally hardwired with gifts that help us become Shepherds, Trawlermen, Police officers, Nurses, and suchlike. Throughout our lives, we seek out education to help us achieve those dreams. So it is up to us to educate and direct our dog's innate instincts to be the best pet, sport, or service dog they could be. We must tap into their desires and give them an outlet for their breed. Unfortunately, we may try and fit a square peg into a round hole with our dogs, as we do with people. However, we can rub off some of those edges with game-based training. We can achieve harmony once again in our pet dog household. Likewise, if you are training a support and service dog to have extraordinary skills, these game plans are the place to start.

We could become the victim in our story and lament that our dog had a poor experience when he was a puppy. We could even be the villain of their story by using harsh punishment when training our dogs. Instead, let's be heroes for our dogs so they can be our superhero sidekicks.

Hero dog owners get things done by visualising what they want their dogs to achieve. They search for new games on their quest to achieve their goals. They aim for incremental breakthrough improvements, not perfection, as in the myth of a perfect dog, just like Lassie. They also know their problems and challenges are just steps on their journey.

Vision game plans can be enough to create a new perspective, helping us to communicate more fully with our dogs. They move us from the known problem story to the adventure of the unknown and what might be. Vision game plans help us see how our concern over our dog's behaviour serves us on our quest. We can see what our dog is telling us, for, after all, our dogs are only what we have taught them and what they practise in the environment in which we have put them. Therefore, by noting our dog's behaviours, we can live each day intentionally training new skills for our dogs to learn.

Since adopting planning for myself and my dogs, my life has been given a new story. I realised that by writing down a projected storyline for Joy, I could see how much more we, as a team, could be and how the success of her story is wrapped up with mine. Using story writing techniques, I could see that I had the agency to effect change in her life and, at the same time, improve my own. Why not join me on such a quest? Link your dream to the reality of the dog in front of you.

Below, I give step-by-step guidance with my own example of Joy's game-based training plans. I start with a six-year plan, then a three-year and one-year projected vision worksheet and then make a daily plan for the activities I need to take on to make things happen. Have a go yourself. But most of all, have fun with your dog as you learn good dogmanship while teaching your hero dog sidekick. Happy Training, dear reader!

Joy's Projected Life Story

Yvonne, her owner, bought Joy to be a P.A.T. Dog (Pets as therapy dog) for her mother, who lived in a care home. Joy was a loving and trustworthy dog, great with both the old and the young. She did her job well, and after Yvonne's mother died, Joy had a new life to lead in the wilds of the Kent countryside. Yvonne decided that as Joy had a high working drive, she would reassign Joy's energy towards competitive obedience and heelwork to music activities. Joy enjoyed Monday nights at the dog club and made many new friends. She also picked up the odd rosette for excellent behaviour. Although Joy was not a Border Collie, she was still given high scores for accuracy and poise, giving the competition a run for their money. However, Yvonne was most proud of how Joy conducted herself around Yvonne's grandchildren.

Indeed, with training, Joy learned to be gentle and polite around all ages. In her later years, Joy accompanied Yvonne on school talks, where she helped children understand how they should behave around dogs.

My Dog's Projected Story

107

Joy's Six-Year Game-Plan Worksheet	Age Thirteen Years
My Activities	**Family Activities**
P.A.T. Dog Training (trained from puppyhood) substituted with new activities	Daily walks with family
Competition obedience dog training	Family outings to dog-friendly venues
Heelwork to Music training	Socialisation with the smallest members of the family
Ambassador Dog for Yvonne's Talks and displays	
Retirement Job for Joy - reading with kids [34]	

Dog's Activities	My Dog's Breed Needs
Herding / Hunting	**Herding / Hunting**
Catch me game	Joy has a strong prey drive - she loves to hunt and follow scent trails. Birds are her favourite. So we will play lots of hunting games to redirect her energies.
Check Back game (recall from a distance)	
Scent trails	
Premack games [35]	

Social Contact	Social Contact
Learning to stand whilst grooming	Joy is a particularly cuddly dog - she loves social contact and being groomed.
Boundary games	
Manner's game	

Eating	Eating
Using Joy's daily food ration for games above	All dogs love to eat, but because Joy has a high prey drive, I will use her daily food ration in a more creative way to fulfil her need to hunt. [36]

Chewing	Chewing
Using stuffed bones and chews for calming activity during the day - after exciting events and as a wind-down activity before bedtime.	Chewing is a calming activity that dogs need - some more than others. But Joy loves to chew.

Play	Play
I will Play the games above (and others that I discover she enjoys) regularly and use coffee breaks as a reminder to play with Joy throughout the day.	Play is essential for dogs, as it is part of an inbuilt system in their brain - to seek out and enjoy novelty. No one understands the function of this system yet, but it shows the emotional state of Joy. [37]

Rest and Sleeping	*Rest and Sleeping* [38]
Allocate times for rest - especially when grandchildren visit.	*I shall note how long she is given time to rest. Joy makes good choices when she has had sufficient rest. Having rest times is especially important when I have the grandchildren around.*
Use the outside run to give Joy a break from the attention of the children.	
Use baby gates and pens to allow separation from the constant attention of children.	

[34] *As a grandmother and an ex-English teacher I think this will be a lovely job for Joy in her retirement. Although dogs like us become slower in their old age we can still give them a job to do that helps their mental wellbeing. Dogs still love to work and be involved in life. Retirement is not only an issue for us, but it is an issue for our dogs too.*

[35] *These are games where I ask Joy to engage in an activity with me and then I allow her to do a behaviour that she really likes as a reward. Which means she is more likely to carry out the behaviour again. Premack was a Professor of psychology who discovered this principle.*

[36] *Hiding food and creating scent trails is one example of games I might play with Joy.*

[37] *A dog that is depressed, frightened, or angry will not play.*

[38] *Dogs need up to seventeen hours of sleep a day (whatever the breed). A tired and stressed dog will make poor choices.*

Joys Three-Year Game-Plan Worksheet [39]	Age Ten Years
My Activities	*Family Activities*
Dog Club - taking her Good Citizen Awards.	Walks with family - allowing grandchildren to hold the lead (using double lead for safety)
Obedience Training for fun	
Heelwork to Music Training for fun [40]	

Dog's Activities	My Dog's Breed Needs
Herding / Hunting	*Herding / Hunting*
Scent Games Programme - online course	Scent Games
Activities as laid out by the Kennel Club's Good Citizen Award Scheme [41]	Whip it Games for fun [44]

Social Contact	Social Contact
Train Joy to allow grooming and be handled by a third party - training for examination by the vet. [42]	Grooming and handling.

Eating	Eating
Daily ration used for training.	Seeking and finding food activities.

Chewing	Chewing
Using stuffed bones and chews for calming activity during the day - after exciting events and as a wind-down activity before bedtime.	Essential Breed Need.

Play	Play
Training Programme [43]	Play and training become 'one and the same.'

Rest and Sleeping	Rest and Sleeping
Review Joy's rest - especially on busy days.	Seventeen hours per day.

Health Goals	Care and Grooming
Healthy eating (little and often - Joy is a deep-chested dog and could be prone to gastric torsion - twisting of the stomach)	Keep up to date with vaccinations.
Balance games and fitness training	Regular grooming sessions at least once a week
Find a good Hydrotherapy Centre	Check and file nails at least once a week

Social Goals	Things ... will do every day
Join my Church Social Walks with other dogs	AM Walk or Training
Dog Club Nights	PM Walk or Training

[39] *The Three-Year Game-Plan is more specific and measurable.*

[40] *You may want to take your training up to competition level or to achieve a Level Three certificate with Dog A.I.D. a charity that helps owners train their own service dogs.*

[41] *Training activities all will tap into Joy's high prey drive, and by satisfying her need to use this part of her brain I will achieve a calmer dog.*

[42] *This is part of the Good Citizen Awards, and though Joy is seven years old, we have never had to have a third party examine her as my husband has always been her vet. However, I suggest you don't leave it as long as I have.*

[43] *See Weekly and Daily Game-Plan Worksheets.*

[44] *Both Scent and Whip games can be found on my You Tube Channel.*

Joys One - Year Game-Plan Worksheet	Age Eight Years
My Activities	Family Activities
Dog Club - Pass Bronze/Silver Award.	Walks with family (Grandchildren are not quite old enough to hold the lead yet, but getting Joy used to the idea of little people.)
Obedience Training for fun.	
Heelwork to Music Training for fun.	

Dog's Activities	My Dog's Breed Needs
Herding / Hunting	Herding / Hunting
Research the activities laid out by the Kennel Club's Good - Citizen Award Scheme.	Scent Games for fun
Play scent games for fun	Whip it games for fun

Social Contact	Social Contact
Train Joy to allow grooming and be handled by a third party - training for examination by the vet.	Grooming and handling.

Eating	Eating
Daily ration used for training.	Seeking and finding food activities.

Chewing	Chewing
Calming Times with Chews etc.	Essential Breed Need.
Using stuffed bones and chews for calming activity during the day - after exciting events and as a wind-down activity before bedtime.	

Play	Play
Training Programme [45]	Play and training become 'one and the same.'

Rest and Sleeping	Rest and Sleeping
Review Joy's rest - especially on busy days.	Seventeen hours per day.

Health Goals	Care and Grooming
Healthy eating (little and often - Joy is a deep-chested dog and could be prone to gastric torsion - twisting of the stomach)	Keep up to date with vaccinations.
Balance games and fitness training	Regular grooming sessions at least once a week
Find a good Hydrotherapy Centre	Check and file nails at least once a week. [46]

Social Goals	Things … will do every day
Join my Church Social Walks with other dogs	AM Walk or Training
Dog Club Nights	PM Walk or Training

[45] See Weekly and Daily Game Plan Worksheets.

[46] I use a Pet Nail Grinder to file my dogs' nails at least once a week, but if you use nail clippers this should be done every six weeks. You should take care not to cut too short as this will cut into the quick of the dog's nails.

___ *Year Game-Plan Worksheet* [47]	*Age _____ Years*
My Activities	*Family Activities*

Dog's Activities	*My Dog's Breed Needs* [48]
Herding / Hunting	*Herding / Hunting*

Social Contact	*Social Contact*

Eating	*Eating*

Chewing	*Chewing*

Play	Play

Rest and Sleeping	Rest and Sleeping

Health Goals	Care and Grooming

Social Goals	Things … will do every day

[47] Make a six-year, three-year and one-year game plan.

[48] Research what your dog needs so that you can create your dog's activities to align with those needs.

Goal Setting Game - Plan Worksheet [49]	Dog's Name Joy	Breed and Age Leonberger - Seven Years
Goal Name		Deadline
Award-Winning Pet Dog		15 June 2025

Describe this Goal	Why does the goal matter - to you!	Daily Steps
Have a dog that has passed all the Good Citizen Awards.	I want Joy beside me as a demo dog during my talks.	I will take the time to play and train with Joy.
Build my dog's confidence to cope with different environments.	Achieving the goal would mean I had a dog that could accompany me anywhere (if appropriate) and be a dog that lives up to her name, Joy.	I shall be intentional about what I teach her every moment of the day.
Have a dog that is good with the grandchildren.	I am aware that children can over excite dogs and it is important to keep my granddaughters' safe.	After all, dogs learn from everything in their environment. So isn't it better to teach her to live in harmony with the family?

Name Three Goal Partners		
My Husband	My Daughter	My Coach

Breakthroughs [50]		
1. Pass Bronze Citizen Awards	2. Pass Silver Citizen Awards	3. Pass Gold Citizen Awards

Daily Steps [51]		
Twenty Mins Training Every Day. Each day schedule three games for three weeks to establish the desired behaviour.	*Film Daily Training to discuss with my Coach weekly.*	*At least one hour of exercise a day. Exercise can be a dog walk, fitness training or a trip to the hydrotherapy pool.*

[49] *Mindset is essential to achieving goals and having clarity about your goals will make you more likely to succeed. Having a coach you are accountable to will also spur you on. They will be invested in your success and will give you help along the way with your journey.*

[50] *For Dog A.I.D. Clients this is an ideal opportunity to write down your commitment to reaching Level Three and qualify your dog as a fully-fledged assistant dog.*

[51] *The twenty minutes can be split up into five-minute sessions throughout the day - our dogs learn 24/7 so the aim is to be intentional about what your train. If you are preparing a meal you can use this session to train a calm stay on their boundary bed.*

Goal Setting Game - Plan Worksheet [52]	Dog's Name _____	Breed and Age _____
Goal Name		Deadline

Describe this Goal	Why does the goal matter - to you!	Daily Steps

Name Three Goal Partners		

Breakthroughs [53]		
1.	2.	3.

Daily Steps		

[52] Mindset is essential to achieving goals and giving clarity, you will be more likely to succeed. Having an accountability partnership with a coach will also spur you on. Your coach will be invested in your success and will give you help along the way with your journey.

[53] For Dog A.I.D. Clients this is an ideal opportunity to write down your commitment to reaching Level 3 and qualify your dog as a fully-fledged assistant dog.

Daily Game - Planner	Dog on a Mission - Date 17 June 2022
My Morning Ritual **Read my dog's Projected Story -** Yes **Read my Game-Plan Worksheets -** Yes **Read my Goals -** Yes	**If I could relive this day, how would I do things differently?** Robert went out, and I could have used his arrival back home as an opportunity to cue Joy to go to her bed.
Primary Game One [54] 'Bub Bub' Game [55]	**Three Things that show improvement** • More focused on me.
Primary Game Two Collar Grab Game	▪ Getting a quicker response by offering her collar.
Primary Game Three Recall from ten paces Game	▪ No longer getting up before the free cue.

Secondary Games and Daily Management		Your Schedule for the day	
My Activity	**Dog's Activity**	**Time**	**Your Activity plus Plan for Your Dog**
Zoom Call and writing time	Calmness [56]	9 am - 10.45 am	Writing – whilst Joy potters about with Robert in the garden
Going for a Walk	'Can you wait?' game (polite behaviour around doors). Transition games	10.45 am - 11.30 am	Include some hill walking for fitness for both my dog and my health.
Coffee Break and a Zoom call	Calming Chew on Boundary	11.30 am - 12.30 pm	Ask Joy to sit with me in the office, ready for Zoom with Dog A.I.D client – Joy is ready to

			demo if needed.
Lunch, then time for writing	*Joy chilling out – pottering around the house*	*12.30 pm - 6 pm*	*Whilst having lunch and writing Joy takes a nap.*
Focus on Joy's Training – Then watch some T.V.	*Playing with me – as training for Joy is fun*	*6 pm - 10 pm*	*Enjoy focussed time with Joy, then chill out watching T.V. before bedtime.*

[54] *Each of the primary Games I will play for three weeks to establish the desired behaviour - I make a note when I started and project forward three weeks and make a note in my diary to review my progress.*

[55] *This game can be found on my YouTube Channel.*

[56] *This can be achieved - see section on Calmness Protocols and games*

Daily Game - Planner	Dog on a Mission - Date _____
My Morning Ritual *Read my dog's Projected Story - ___* *Read my Game-Plan Worksheets -* ___ *Read my Goals - ___*	*If I could relive this day, how would I do things differently?*
Game One	*Three Things that show improvement*
Game Two	
Game Three	

Secondary Games and Daily Management		Your Schedule for the day [57]	
My Activity	*Dog's Activity*	*Time*	*Your Activity plus plan for Your Dog*

[57] *Your daily schedule should include how you might manage your dogs during the activity.*

Remember the Three for Three Rule

When planning daily schedules, choose three games you will play to arrive at the desired behaviour of your dog training goal. Map out three weeks and make a date when you are going to review the behaviour. Have someone you can be accountable to—that might be a friend, your dog training class, or a dog training coach. Tell them at the beginning of the three weeks what behaviour you aim to achieve. Then film or show off your dog's progress. Having an accountability partner will keep you on track.

Harmony House Management

Follow dog management strategies around the home to create harmony in your household. For example, use baby gates and crates to provide quiet sanctuaries for your dog. A calm refuge is vital in a busy family home because dogs need seventeen hours of sleep. A tired dog will make poor decisions and might result in a child getting bitten by the family's dog.

I can't possibly cover all the breed need games for every type of dog in this book. But I can point you to understanding what category your dog may fall under and how to provide the need for a dog under that heading; for example, Herders, Hunters, Guardian, or Companion dogs.

I have hinted at some propensities throughout the book. Still, I would love every reader to become their dog's ethologist and learn about what their dogs want and need. For example, when we carry out a training game with our dog—that could be sitting to greet a visitor—and something goes wrong, we can look back and evaluate. Our dogs only know what they know, and we have to show them how a training game should look in the environment we have put them in. So as we watch them bouncing all over our visiting friends, we have to ask ourselves why our dog may be doing that. Instead of asking how I can stop my dog's naughty behaviour, we start to try and understand the situation from your dog's point of view. Now we need to ask, what is my dog thinking? The evaluation could be he is unable to think when he is excited. The solution—train him to listen to me even when he is highly enthusiastic. Training games should be played not in the situation but rather for future problems. Rather than train when your dog is bound to fail, it would be kinder to you and your dog to employ a child gate to allow the guest to come in before letting the dog out to greet them. We could even pop our dogs into their crate. Letting your dog out to say hello must only happen when the dog is entirely calm and bored with the whole idea of greeting your guest. Therefore, greeting guests must only occur when we have taught them the correct behaviour. Again, this is when we need to understand ourselves as humans. Listening to friends say they don't mind your puppy jumping up is tempting. But believe me, if you have a large dog like a Leonberger, that would certainly not be the case when they are fully grown. Now is the time to find the courage to say to well-meaning friends and family that you have to insist that they do not allow jumping up.

On the other hand, our dog might be fiddling about and being a clown. Therefore as we evaluate our dog as acting like a complete loon, we might look at his body language. Here, we may recognise that our dog is uncomfortable and is behaving that way because one of the five F's have come into play—fear.[34] This behaviour indicates that your dog is appeasing the guest and telling them he is no threat to them. When our dogs show this behaviour, we need to help them gain confidence around strangers, both in and out of the home. For example, games like 'say hellos' as described at the end of my book.

Then we might ask what our dogs understand when they hear the doorbell ring or a knock on the door. If they start barking immediately, we can then evaluate that this is, for them, a cue for a practised behaviour. The doorbell will trigger the behaviour they chose when the last guest visited. Hoping each visitor will help your dog to be calmer is a recipe for frustration for you and your dog. It's like Einstein's definition of insanity: 'doing the same thing over and over again and expecting different results.' Our dogs only become what they practise. We will not achieve better results when we allow our

---

[34] *Five F's – Fight, Flight, Freeze, Faint, and Fiddle About.*

dogs to get excited when visitors arrive. We may think we are training our dogs. Rather, we are giving them opportunities to practise the behaviour we do not like. When assessing a behaviour we do not want, the first port of call is not training but management. If our dogs cannot greet people calmly, this is when we have to take our leadership role seriously.

As you evaluate your dog's ability to greet a stranger, you will notice one of the steps towards greeting is faulty. For example, right from the beginning, the visitor knocks on the door, the dog should be calm, and you send your dog to his bed whilst you let the guest into the hall. Then you give the cue 'say hellos,' and your dog sniffs the person's shoes and sits to be petted. Each step towards a calm greeting must be split up and practised before being together for a final greeting. We must notice if one of the chains of behaviour leading to a calm sit-to-greet has weakened. Now, this is when you have to practise one portion of the behaviour chain to reach your goal. For example, your dog may find the beginning stage much more exciting than all the following stages. That does not mean you have failed; it just means that you now know the roadblock to your dream outcome. This failure in the chain will help you to move forward to success. The best part is that it allows you to measure your progress too.

You can assess how they have reacted to the doorbell or the knock on the door, and you can set this part of the chain up as a game. You can, if you like, get your partner or friend to knock on the door every time they come into a room, and this becomes the cue for your dog to get into their bed for a treat. I call these my crazy games because anyone watching might think I have lost the plot. But it does pay off if you play the game for three weeks. Then every time the door knocks, your dog will instantly jump on their beds. Now here I have to confess. I rarely get unannounced visitors, and when the door knocks, I have a 'that will do' cue, and they are then asked to go behind a baby gate whilst I accept a package. If I have a scheduled visit from friends, my dogs are mainly in another room and are not let out. This habit started because I had a friend who was scared of dogs. However, I managed to get her to overcome her fears. My friend has recently stayed with me overnight with the dogs, just milling about as they would typically do. But this illustrates how we must evaluate and manage situations for our particular lifestyle. There is no one answer to what you allow your dog to do or not do. However, like me, you might have friends and family who are inwardly terrified of dogs, even if they do not admit it. It is best to consider how a guest's fear might affect your dog and then put management first rather than training. Dogs sense the discomfort of their humans. Although I do not advocate that they will take advantage of that fear, they will pick up on the emotion and mirror the feelings with a behaviour picked from the five F's. What they choose depends on their breed type, temperament, and previous experiences. What we need to do for our dogs is to guard them against fearful encounters and help them make the right choices so that there is harmony in our household.

So how do we help our dogs make the right choices? We need to make our communication with our dogs clear and concise. We do this by playing games with our dogs that help build a good relationship and a clear line of communication.

Remember that your dog might find your interactions punishing, even if you think you are rewarding your dog. For example, when our dog sidles up for attention, we cannot resist giving our dog a big hug. Me included. But we have to teach our dogs to tolerate this unique human behaviour. Hugging is not a sign of affection for dogs but the opposite. An embrace, for dogs, comes before a full-blown disagreement with another dog. Just watch puppies play. You might come across the playful bully who tries out the hugging routine. If he is playing with an older dog, this will only get him in trouble. The older dog will undoubtedly put him in his place for being very rude. So when we hug our dogs, they will feel completely conflicted. And if you have a high-drive working dog, they will not be interested in a hug when working. A rewarding game or other interaction is a much better reinforcer than any other form of physical contact. However, you might need to try a gentle massage when you need to bring a highly excited working dog's arousal levels down. Hold your dog's collar calmly and massage its shoulders so he relaxes. Utilise massage when your dog has become too excited, especially when children are around.

Good communication is essential if you have a small child in the household. A family often buys a dog with the idea that it will be a perfect companion for their children or even a substitute nanny. Children's stories indeed perpetuate the ideal dog. Just think of the large dog in J. M. Barrie's story and play, *Peter Pan*. On social media, there are now a plethora of videos showing tiny babies nestled between a large dog's paws. It seems that mothers want to show off how loving and caring their dogs are. However, I just cringe. Unfortunately, as a behaviourist, I have seen the results of such unwarranted trust. Children act unpredictably, and dogs can be put in situations that, for them, are seen as threatening, which can end in your child being bitten. The bite can be so quick you will not be able to prevent it. Loving hugs from a toddler will be seen as a threat to your dog. Because the threat is not understood, there are more incidents of children being bitten by a family dog. We must remember that we are humans and love to hug; dogs do not!

I always tell my clients that they should remember the different ways our dogs communicate. Be super vigilant when you mix children with dogs. And don't forget the stress caused to your dog during holidays and family gatherings when emotions are heightened. The dog's routine will have been disrupted, and the frustration might spill over. Frustrated outbursts often occur if they have not had their usual walk. Then, unfortunate outcomes can result when you mix frustration with young children who, like your dog, might not understand impulse control and boundaries. As a grandmother, I always ensure my dogs are kept behind child gates. We romantically think that dogs must be in the same room to feel included. Still, we should keep them out of harm's way so they can enjoy the company of the family from a safe distance. Dogs also need to have a place they can go where they will not be disturbed and should be completely out of the way to unwind and relax. Highly aroused and tired dogs make poor decisions.

So how do we make a line of communication clear to our dogs? It is simple. I carry out a schedule of dog training games that helps my dog understand me and helps them become more flexible about the change in their routine. My game-based training plans teach them 'impulse control' and how to think through and make the right choices.[35] Games also help us to understand our dogs and improve their mental welfare. We can adjust our dog's outlook on life and increase their adaptability to the environment in which we have placed them. Also, by playing games, we will fulfil their breed needs.

---

[35] *Impulse Control, is the ability to think and not carrying out an instinctive behaviour, i.e. for a herding dog not to give chase when it sees movement.*

But, needless to say, play is beneficial for us too. The function of play has not been fully understood as yet. Still, the absence of play shows an animal's emotional state—for example, a depressed, frightened, or angry dog doesn't play.[36] However, this can be remedied. By building up good communication with your dog, through the simple steps in the game plans, you will find your dog will start to come out of its shell. Indeed, you will find your dog will look forward to the game plan schedule.

Food Rations and Training Treats

I often explain to owners that their dogs enjoy working for their food, which is called Contrafreeloading. However, it makes some clients feel uneasy by even thinking about enforcing their beloved pets to work for their food. It would be like telling a child they can't have breakfast until they clean their room. It feels wrong somehow. But we must remember that our dogs were hardwired to hunt out their meal. The SEEKING System in the dog's brain is, I believe, an essential part of the dog's motivations. Jaak Panksepp describes how the SEEKING system in the brain 'leads organisms to eagerly pursue the fruits of their environment—from nuts to knowledge, so to speak. Like other emotional systems, arousal of the SEEKING system has a characteristic feeling tone—

---

[36] *Grandin, Temple and Johnson, Catherine. Animals Make Us Human. New York: Mariner Books, 2010 p. 6–9.*

psychic energisation that is difficult to describe but is akin to that invigorated feeling of anticipation we experience when we actively seek thrills and other rewards. Clearly this type of feeling contributes to many distinct aspects of our active engagement with the world.'[37] Therefore, how can we deny our dogs the anticipatory thrill of seeking out their food?

Without this thrill, many dogs are in a state of depression, especially those with closer genetic links to working stock. So I always advise clients to use their dog's daily ration to help satisfy their dog's desire for food and the experience of the hunt. I gently introduce a puzzle food dispenser instead of a bowl for some clients. Still, as they get used to the idea that their dog enjoys hunting for their food, they can use the dog's daily ration for scent games around the house where a trail of food is left, so their dog can seek the food out. If you use wet food, small amounts can be stuffed into a rubber toy food dispenser and placed around the house. When you go out, your dog hunting out for food alleviates anxiety. Instead of your dog feeling anxious when you go out, they will get excited as they will see it as a cue for dinner time. After hunting for their food, they will settle down for a nap. However, for multi-dog households, this is not a game I would recommend for when you go out. Rather stuff a rubber toy with their food and place it in each of the dog's crates. Giving food in their crates will

---

[37] Panksepp, Jaak *Affective Neuroscience: The Foundations of Human and Animal Emotions. E-book.* New York: Oxford University Press, 1998 p. 5317

stop any desire for competitiveness between your dogs, resulting in a heated argument where one dog might get hurt.

Don't forget to measure your dog's daily food ration and use about 60% for training. However, when you are out and about, you will have to use a higher value of training treat. Treats could be shop-bought, or you could use leftover chicken from your Sunday roast. When out and about, you will find their ordinary kibble will not be enough wages for them to think about not seeking out something better in their environment. The simple way to prevent this is by playing distraction games. You, as the owner, must transmit all the value of the SEEKING system to you and make it work in your favour.

House Training

When you get a new puppy, don't forget they are still very young and may not be able to go through the night without needing to relieve themselves. You need to help your puppy know where the toilet is and build up the time between wanting to go and getting to the designated spot you have chosen in the garden. Adult rescue dogs also might need guidance regarding the correct toileting places.

Here are some top tips to speed up potty training.

1. Never tell your puppy or dog off when they make a mistake, as it will slow down the potty-training process.

2. Puppies and dogs rarely soil their beds unless they are sick. If you make their beds comfy and soft, put them in a puppy crate, and give them at least one toilet break in the night, they will soon get the idea of where they should go to the bathroom.

3. During the day, watch out for circling and sniffing, which usually indicates they are about to do a wee or a poo. When you see your puppy circle, immediately pick them up and put them on the spot in the garden you have dedicated for them to use as their toilet. Wait a while saying, "*hurry-up*," as they probably get too interested in sniffs to go immediately. Once they remember they wanted to wee, your puppy will eventually perform, and you can give them a treat saying what a good puppy they are.

4. Always remember a puppy usually wants to go to the toilet after a nap or eating. After eating, most puppies like to have a poo, so when you take them out, say "*be quick*" and give them a treat when they perform.

5. During the day, let your puppy out every hour, saying, "*hurry-up*" or "*be quick*"—"*hurry-up*" is a cue for a wee, and "*be quick*" is the cue for a poo. So handily, when you go on holiday, they will perform on your signal! (For those whose puppy is now fully grown, you can still teach them to go on cue by saying the cue words when you are sure they are about to go to the

toilet. Then give them a treat as a reward. They will soon learn to go on your signal no matter how old they are.) Nobody will know what you are asking them to do, and it is much less embarrassing than saying, "*go wee wees*" or "*go poo-poos.*"

6. Give them at least ten minutes if they do not perform on cue straight away. If your puppy has not been successful, take them back into the house, be vigilant, and try again in another ten minutes.

7. Always accompany your dog on their toilet breaks, and remember to play a game with them after they have been successful.

8. If you can't supervise your puppy at any time, to avoid mistakes—put them in a puppy pen with puppy pads to soak up the wees and poos. You can even make a puppy toilet with a litter tray filled with soil or grass, just like a cat. It speeds up potty training, as dogs learn dirt or grass is the place to wee or poo. But eventually, they will know to do it anywhere on cue, which is helpful if you are at a service station on a trip. But don't forget to bag any poo and put it in a bin.

Troubleshooting

If your puppy comes in from a toilet break and decides to wee or poo in front of you, pick him up and take him calmly outside to continue, even if your puppy is in mid-flow. If you stay vigilant and catch them in the act, your puppy will soon realise that weeing or pooing inside is not wanted. Remember, do not scold your dog. It will only slow the training down.

What a Difference a Breed Makes

As I have said earlier, clients often complain that their dog does not want to play with them or take food from their hands. Breeds have different preferences for games and interactions. But be assured that relationships are crucial to your dog as they are to the human being on the other end of the lead. Therefore, before we even think about training our dogs, we must consider their breed needs and how they like interacting with their humans and other dogs.

For example, each breed type has a specific preference for touch. Herding breeds are often touch sensitive, especially around their feet. Breeders have selected touch sensitivity so that the dog is responsive and can get out of the way of a kick from livestock whilst it is herding. Herding breeds also like to play games at a distance and will feel under pressure if you use a short tuggy toy. I often use a tug on the end of a long line for a herding type breed, as they find it more comfortable to play further away from your hand.

Guardian breeds also have different needs, for example, when it comes to playing and being touched. They love to be touched and handled. With my own Leonberger, she will lean into me for extra contact. This has been useful, as I have now used the cue 'steady me' since I suffer from bouts of vertigo. However, she is still a genetically driven dog to guard our territory. Here, I must be vigilant as this will sadly cause issues if unchecked. Her guarding behaviours will worsen if I do not meet my Guardian breed's needs. For example, allowing her to fight with another dog on the other side of the fence might result in her redirecting her frustration towards a family member. As a grandmother, I cannot afford to be complacent. Therefore, the answer for guarding breeds is to play games where they learn that coming away from the fence will not be the end of their fun but the beginning of a game with you. That is why I put the 'Chase me' games on the top of my list for the guarding breed.[38] In my experience with my own Leonberger, toy and treat motivation were not high on her list of likes. Although, she loved to be cuddled. But a cuddle will not be enough motivation when she is in full fence guarding mode. Therefore, I have included in her daily routine a set of games. Joy is allowed to tell me that we have someone (in her opinion) too close to the fence. Then I expect her to return when called and given the 'that will do' cue. As a dog who loves cuddles, I also ensure that we include massage in her daily routine.

Because of my experience with my Leonberger, I often advise clients who have problems with their dog in regards to

---

[38] *See 'Chase Me' Game*

play to start by stroking and handling their dog. Give your dog some spa time, where you massage them gently. Start with a puppy, but if you have an adult dog from a rescue, you can start with a programme of massage techniques given to you by a Tellington Touch practitioner.[39] An adult dog may have issues about being touched in certain areas. Whatever the case, your dog needs to trust your hands on their body. I know only too well that dogs must be handled for veterinary procedures. So for my husband, being both our dogs' vet and owner, he had to develop inventive ways to keep our dogs' trust and still carry out procedures that needed to be done. However, this is a subject for another book. Needless to say, the more you handle your dog, the better it will be for your vet to carry out the procedures that need to be done—for example, massaging the joint where the tail and the spine meet will desensitise your dog to anal gland exams. When your dog drags its bottom on the floor, it might signal that they need emptying, and you will require your vet to empty the glands for you. Another routine is to scruff the back of your dog's neck to get them used to the idea of being scruffed when given their routine injections. When I first got my Border Collie thirteen years ago, there was a lot about not putting your hands on the dog whilst training. This philosophy pushed the pendulum far too far in the wrong direction.

---

[39] *Practitioners | TTouch Training British Isles*

Dogs should be used to being handled and touched. However, this should be done without force or coercion. Handling should be done with the cooperation of your dog. Sarah Fisher was one of the first TTouch practitioners who understood the idea of animal-centred care. Many ACE-certified trainers have helped other pet professionals to understand kind handling approaches. These handling methods help your dog understand that your hands mean no harm.[40] However, even if you are not a TTouch practitioner, you can simply massage around your dog's shoulders whilst gently holding your dog's collar. Massage can be beneficial for calming a dog when it is over-excited and finds it too challenging to bring its own arousal level down again.

Hunting dogs, including the hounds and gun dogs, are dogs whose breed needs cannot be ignored. Owners who do not give their dog sufficient outdoor activities under their guidance will find that their dog has a propensity to engage in unwanted behaviours. These undesirable behaviours may not necessarily come out in hunting behaviours per se. Such as the dog wanting to chase after a critter. That is just the tip of the iceberg for a dog who desires to hunt. Failure to provide the proper outlet for these dogs' needs may include stereotypies of pacing and tail-chasing. They may even show other persistent behaviours—for example, self-mutilation. Sadly,

---

[40] *Tilley Farm What is TTouch*

my husband has had to remove tails in the most severe cases. Frustration might even lead to fence guarding, constantly vigilant and unable to rest. That is why Joy, my Leonberger, is not allowed to stay outside unattended. I am only too aware she does not truly relax, which may lead later to health problems. For the hunting dog, scent games will save them from lack of environmental stimulation, which can lead to the issues I have listed. These dogs need to follow scent trails set up by the owner.[41] They also need to put the 'go sniff' on cue so that the owner is not dragged down the street by a dog who has gained the scent trail of some wild critter they want to follow at any cost.

You may believe the Toy and Companion breeds will not cause an owner any heartache. After all, they have been bred to love sitting on our lap and being close companions. But do not be fooled by those big adorable eyes. These dogs may have been bred to look like children, and they may permanently act like juvenile puppies. Still, they come with a whole set of problems associated with this breeding. Not only is their health affected by the shortening of their noses to make them look more human, but we have bred them to want to be close to their human at all times. Therefore, many of those in the Companion dog category find being separated from their own too much to bear. We need to give these dogs the

---

[41] *See Scent Games*

confidence to cope with being alone. Playing games boosts their confidence and ability to work out things for themselves—finding food scattered in boxes or retrieving keys that rattle all help. Try and be inventive, and if you find you are running out of ideas, get in touch with me, and I will direct you to the Netflix™ of dog training games.

Game-Plan Games to Add to Your Worksheets

Collar Grab Game

The Collar Grab game helps with lots of problems around the house. I condition all my dogs to know when my hand goes towards their collar, a treat will follow. My dogs then automatically drop what is in their mouth or turn to me if I just want them to change direction.

1. Grab your dog's collar. The grab must not be harsh, and you must not be tempted to jerk at it angrily if your dog has stolen an item in the house. Instead, it should be done calmly.

2. As your dog looks up at you, say, "Yes."

3. Then immediately give your dog a treat.

Distraction Game Level One

Every dog is vigilant to new information. What your dogs see, hear, smell, taste, or want to touch all play a part in environmental distractions. The value of that distraction depends on the dog's genetics and past experience, as well as the distance away and any perceived movement. For my dog Fred, blackbirds are his nemesis. He will really kick off if he sees a blackbird. Therefore, to compete with environmental distractions, I have to play games where these distractions are less likely to happen. The mantra for all games is to play the game first and test whether you have succeeded in being more interesting than the environment around you.

1. Set up a mild distraction for your dog in the garden, which could be as simple as having a helper roll a ball across their path.

2. Every time your helper rolls the ball, and your dog notices it, say calmly, "good" and give him a treat for re-engaging with you. The words "good" or "yes" should already be a cue for your dog that a treat is about to follow.

3. Now make the distraction more difficult by rolling the ball closer to your dog. If he pulls to try and get at the ball, you have pushed the game on too quickly. Go back to rolling the ball further away from you. But don't forget to say calmly, "good" and give him the treat.

4. Now that you have set your dog up to understand the game, you can transfer this to any distraction. You could go to a quiet road and wait for cyclists or joggers to pass. When they take notice of these environmental

distractions, don't forget to say "good" and treat them straight away.

5. Eventually, your dog will understand that you are the only one they should focus on when they are out and about. However, if your dog gets excited about meeting new people, play the game below.

Say Hellos Game

I do not always let my dogs out when we have guests, so they learn that it is not their business to take centre stage when I have a visitor. I always train for the situation and not in the situation. Training for the situation means we practise 'meet and greet' with like-minded friends. As the dog jumps, ask your friend only to pet your dog if it is calm. I then train each section of the meet and greet sequence separately.

1. I play the game—automatic sit. This game is played on the lead, and you ask your dog to sit when you stop.

2. Now you play guess when I stop with your dog. The guessing game is played by walking in a figure of eight, then circles, and now and again stop when they least expect it. When you stop, they should automatically sit.

3. Then I play recall games when you send your dog to a family member and then have them recall back to you.

4. Now you are ready to play the say hello game with the visitors that have arranged a specific time to come to

your house. But remember, it should be played as a game, and you should not nag them to get off when they try to jump up. Playing this game will help your dog learn to listen to you while excited. However, you must give your dog clear criteria to follow. For example, sit on your bed when the doorbell rings and allow the guest to walk into the room. Only get off the bed when given the cue 'free,' and only meet the guest when given the signal 'say hellos' (which means go and sit in front of the guest to be petted). Then immediately call your dog back to your side. However, play this game on a lead at first. Allow your dog to say hello, and then call them back to you even if they are too excited to sit at first—then send them back to say hello again. Eventually, your dog will catch on to the fact that he doesn't get to be petted when he is too excited.

5. I will often introduce a retrieve game to the scenario with a retriever breed, especially with a mouthy puppy. I used this game when I realised that my elderly parents had fragile skin and tiny puppies' teeth were causing them to bleed, but I said to my dog, "show your toy," as they walked through the front door. However, I made sure they were also happy to have the toy taken off them with the Swapsies game, which I explain below.

Swapsies

When the dog is young, have them attached to a long line to prevent your dog from taking stolen items to a hiding place. Then play games where your dog learns to swap an item for a valued treat or another toy.

1. Start by playing with a tuggy toy, and allow your puppy to pull on the toy. Then let that toy go dead, and then produce another toy for your dog to play with— the toy you play with must always be animated.

2. Your puppy will then automatically go for the animated toy.

3. You can also throw a treat away from the dog to end the game with the cue 'that will do.'

4. Once your dog has the idea that when you produce a toy or food, your dog will always lose interest in the item in its mouth. At that point, I add the cue swapsies.

5. This game satisfies your dog's needs to carry out tasks, including bringing back anything they might have acquired for themselves. It also makes resource guarding issues much more manageable.[42] Because when they have stolen something, you can give the cue swapsies, and they will invariably bring it back to you.

---

[42] *But, if you have children in the family and a dog that shows the propensity to resource guard, I strongly suggest you get in touch with a dog behaviourist.*

I also like to play the 'Get It' game and the 'Think About It' game at this point (see below). I play these games because guests inevitably put things like bags on the floor. I once had a dog who enjoyed sniffing in any guest's belongings to see what she could find. It was pretty embarrassing when she started running about the lounge with the handbag around her head.

Troubleshooting

Clients often tell me their dog does not like treats or toys, and they find it very difficult to motivate them to play. Thus, they find it more challenging to play the games that stop the puppy from going self-employed because their dog has grown used to making their own entertainment—pinching the T.V. remote control or their slippers. These clients tell me that the swapsies game does not work. For this reason, playing with your dog is vital from the day you get them home. You build up the relationship with your dog from day one. Don't let them cry it out when you leave them on the first night in the kitchen. Instead, sleep in the kitchen with them on a camp bed. Or put their crate next to you in your bedroom.

Consequently, your dog will learn to trust you from day one. Also, I never allow food or toys to be down for my dogs to access during the day. I use toys and food to show them that I am the provider of all that is fun. I teach them that all interactions with me are with food and toys from the start. If you have a dog that looks at you blankly when you try and play with them, don't panic. Start a new regime where the relationship with you is the most important thing for your dog. Take up the food from the kitchen floor and use 60% of their food ration for their training. Your dog will then start to look to you for comfort and food. Start simply by putting the allocation in a puzzle bowl if they are refusing food that is not in a bowl. Then introduce a food trail to get to the bowl you can hide for them to find. Be inventive. Games with their food are part of building a relationship with you. I also use toys in their puppy pen to indicate that I am leaving, and they can entertain themselves for a short time whilst I am away.[43]

Time away should be only between five to thirty minutes for small puppies and increased incrementally to three hours maximum when they are adults. If you are taking in a rescue dog, the same rules apply. Do not worry. You will soon be able to teach them to be left alone if you use the puppy or dog pen throughout the day. Gradually work up to your dog staying in the puppy pen for extended periods. Also, do not allow your dog to follow you from room to room. Sadly, separation issues are one of the most significant problems I deal with daily in my behaviour practice. Separation anxiety disorders cannot fully be covered in this book, but suffice it to

---

[43] *Remember to choose safe toys that cannot be destroyed and ingested by your dog, causing a choking hazard or intestinal blockage.*

say if you are experiencing issues, seek a behaviourist's help. But remember that play often overcomes many dogs' anxieties, and games can help build their confidence. My favourite game is Tug.

Tug Training

I teach a puppy that I'm much more fun than anything. Puppies up to sixteen weeks love to keep close. But like any toddler, a dog will gain confidence and want to investigate independently or even chase the neighbour's cat or a squirrel out on a walk. Your puppy may even, more embarrassingly, want to race after someone on a bicycle or a jogger.

Here are some top tips to be more exciting than all these things and have your dog stay close when there are distractions.

Playing Tug Games with Your Puppy or Dog
1. I like my puppy to realise that within a three-foot circumference around me—the average length of a lead—is much more fun than going off and chasing after the neighbour's cat. I also ensure that I allow them to fulfil the need to hunt—which is hardwired into every dog—by playing lots of chasing the toy games.

2. Find the Right Toy—Each dog breed will enjoy a different toy. Puppies like toys with different textures so they can have a choice. For example, a hunting dog

REDISCOVER JOY WITH YOUR DOG

like a working spaniel might like a shaggy dog toy that mimics the feathers of a bird, and a collie might pick a ball on the end of their tug.

3. Choose the right time when your puppy is full of energy, not right after a walk when all they just want is to chill out and cool down.

4. Once the dog has the tug, play a quick pulling game, always pulling your puppy forward.

5. Never push the toy into your puppy's face. Instead, make the toy act like an animal running away.

6. Always have a second toy; when your dog pulls on one toy, let it go dead and make the second toy come alive. By making one toy act like it is jumping and leaving the second toy to become static, you will teach your puppy to let go of toys when you want them to stop the game.

Troubleshooting

Puppies can get overtired, often manifested by zoomies and puppy biting. When you play this game, your puppy might get over-excited and grab at your clothes or nip your fingers when you feed them. Just say, "ouch," and stop playing the game immediately. Wait till your puppy calms down before playing with them again, but if they get over-excited and go zooming around the lounge, then put your puppy in their pen for a rest.

Whip It Game

1. Use a fur lure or one of the dog's tuggy toys attached to a horsewhip.

2. Trail the lure around and make it act like a squirrel.

3. Let your dog have the joy of catching it quickly to create the desire to chase the lure. Many people make the mistake of trying to get their dog to chase around them several times as the dog follows the lure.

4. Build up the chase in layers. The pursuit of the lure can be increased in difficulty and duration as you build up the drive towards the lure. Do not be tempted to leap into a high-powered chase on your first attempts at the game.

5. Wait for an opportunity to whip the lure away from your dog, then immediately start the game again.

6. Some dogs will like to parade around you like a horse on a lunge line—let them do that. It is all part of the fun for them.

7. Wait for the moment the dog releases the lure, then whip it away from them and start the chase again until they recapture the lure.

8. As the game progresses, you can add impulse control by asking for a sit or a down before giving the cue to 'get it.'

Troubleshooting

If you have trouble getting them to release the lure:

1. Ask them to pop up on a boundary bed.

2. Then sprinkle some treats on the bed, at the same time as saying, 'drop.'

3. Let the lure go dead by walking along the line till you reach the lure.

4. Then hold your dog's collar gently, and if you have played collar grab games, they will happily relinquish the lure. But remember to start the game again to reinforce the drop. Or give them a tasty treat and say your cue, indicating it is the end of the game. I always use the cue, 'that'll do.'

5. The 'Whip It' game is a skill that will get better in time for you and your dog. After practise, you will soon find your own ways to bring the game to an end. I often suggest to clients that they practise first without their dog to get their mechanics right. Like swinging the lure towards them and catching it.

Scent Games

Scent games could take up another book in itself as a subject, but suffice it to say, playing scent games will change your dog's mood for the better. It is handy for calming the excitable dog, as scent work involves concentration. As your dog focuses on the scent, their innate instincts kick into place, fulfilling the breed need of dogs such as spaniels. The gun dog (hunting category of dog) notoriously wants to have their nose to the ground.

I start every puppy on games that involve searching for their dinner. This game builds their confidence and shows them the game's goal: to search. Then you can apply the search cue to other games in the future.

1. Begin the game around the house. Start by having your dog beside you, then throw a treat away from you and say the cue; "search."

2. Progress the game to the next level by making a trail around your house of treats they can find under pillows, behind plant pots, etc. Always give permission to start the hunt by giving the cue, 'search.'

Searching for a Person

1. Get a helper to scatter some treats on the ground in a trail and get them to hide. The game can be played first in the home or the garden.

2. Progress the game to out and about, but attach a long line to the dog's harness. A long line allows your dog plenty of scope for following the trail but will keep the dog from rushing ahead and losing you.

3. Follow your dog to the missing person as they gobble

each treat along the trail. Praise them as you go along.

4. When your dog reaches your helper, get them to play the dog's favourite tuggy game. Or the helper could give your dog a jackpot treat (something of high value, such as a leftover slice of beef from your Sunday roast).

5. If you haven't got a helper, you could set up a trail, place a pencil case with the jackpot treat inside, and find the prize together.

6. Eventually, you can dispense with the trail of treats to the prize (a person or a pencil case). As soon as you say search, they will be eager to find the prize and be able to follow the person's scent. Amazingly, they can pick up a person's scent left as they walk towards their hiding place or where the pencil case was left. But remember to track back on the same route to the pencil case; otherwise, you will confuse your dog with two trails.

Troubleshooting

For some dogs going away from you might be scary, especially for the Companion breed who are not confident about working alone. The scent game can also help build a nervous dog's grit for the pressures of the busy urban life.

1. Use old packing boxes from home deliveries and make a pile of them in the middle of the living room.

2. Scatter part of their daily food ration around and in the boxes and let them search the treats out.

3. Once they are having fun finding their dinner, you can add the cue, 'search.' Remember that the puppy or dog must look like he enjoys the game before adding any cue.

Think About It Games versus 'Leave It.'

Most of the time, as humans, we are thinking about how to stop our dogs from doing things. However, most of us want to live in harmony with our dogs and not have to nag them by shouting, "leave it," if they spy on something they want. If the 'Think About It' game is taught correctly, your dog will not dream of scrumping your tasty sandwich from the kitchen counter. And if you teach the 'Get It' game, your dog will only take things you permit them to take. Permission is a powerful tool in our dog training tool kit.

Think About It Game

1. Start by holding some treats in your hand, so your dog can sniff them but can't get the treats.

2. If your dog backs away, open your hand, take a treat with your other hand, and give your dog the treat.

3. If your dog comes in close to your hand again, close your fist around the food.

4. Once your dog can stare at your hand with food in it but make no attempt to steal it, then move on to having treats on the floor. Cup them with your hand when your dog gets close. Wait for your dog to choose to back away, then hand them a treat from the floor.

5. I never put the 'leave it' cue to this game, as not taking something is a concept your dog can't understand. Rather a dog will understand when a game starts and finishes. The game is about understanding the gap between seeing something I want and being permitted to take it.

6. Therefore, progress the 'Think About It' game to include the 'Get It' cue—see below.

Get It Game

1. The 'Get It' game is an extension of the 'Think About it' game. I work up to the point that the dog will stare at a treat on the floor until I give the cue to 'get it.'

2. To start the game, I often use a tuggy, and as I play, I hold the tuggy close to me, and as they pause to think about it, I give them the cue 'get it' and re-introduce the toy to the dog to tug with again.

3. Then I gradually extend the time between the dog disengaging from the toy and being allowed to play with it again on the 'get it' cue.

4. I now transfer this game to the food left on the floor and then give the cue 'get it.'

5. I work up to the point I know that my dogs will stare at the treat until I tell them to 'get it.'

6. Mix up the game of 'Get It' between toys and treats.

7. Every time you play the game, you can extend or shorten the time between the dog staring at the toy or treat before giving them the cue to 'get it.' Keep your dog guessing.

By playing these games regularly, your dog will learn he can only have something when you give him the 'get it' cue. The 'get it' game is handy when you are out on a walk, as they will be focused on you and not pulling you from one sniff to another. You can give them opportunities to 'go sniff' (a cue I use) on a walk so that the dog will only sniff on cue. The 'Go Sniff' game is beneficial for the spaniel, who is known for having its nose on the floor at all times.

The 'Think About It' and 'Get It' games are also helpful when you have visitors to the home, especially children. Playing tuggy and 'Think About It' games will help the dog to be polite around children. However, remember, children may not have learned how to be polite around dogs. Children are naturally drawn to cuddling dogs and love to play with their new puppy. But don't forget that your dog or puppy needs a break from the hustle and bustle of busy family life.

A tired dog will make poor decisions regarding interactions with children.

Greeting Games—Children/Elderly and Puppies/Dogs

The best way to stop a puppy from jumping up is to remember that you must only pet your dog when all four paws are on the ground. Don't forget, when you push a puppy or a dog away from you, they will think you are enjoying the game of them jumping on you and will do it even more.

Here are some top tips to help your dog learn manners around guests:

1. When a puppy jumps up, no matter how friendly the greeting, turn to one side. Your puppy will naturally lose their balance and flop back down onto all four paws—then you can pay attention to your puppy.

2. Train puppies to be calm around visitors—always prepare for a friend's visit rather than trying to train during the visit. Remember to train for the situation, not in the situation. If your puppy is excited, your puppy is not in a state of mind to learn to be calm around guests. We need to train calming games around the house to help your pup to be able to go from the state of being overly excited and then back down to being quiet and well-behaved. When your guest arrives, put your puppy in a playpen and give them a treat if they are calm when you pass by. It also teaches

the pup to cope with being alone. I also throw a treat to the puppy when it is being calm and relaxed when a visitor walks past. The more you practise, the more likely the puppy will calm down when the guest arrives.

3. When your puppy has learned to be calm when you approach the pen, it doesn't matter if they sit or stand as long as all feet are on the ground—you can ask a visitor to come and say hello. However, remember to tell your visitor to walk away as soon as the puppy gets excited.

4. When the puppy becomes calm again, the visitor can approach and treat and stroke your puppy.

5. Always supervise if your visitor is a child and wants to play and cuddle the puppy. Pick your puppy up and take it to the children, but have them sitting on the floor so there is no risk of a child dropping a puppy.

6. Be vigilant, and when your puppy gets too excited and starts nipping at your visitor's hands or feet, remove the puppy and put them in another room.

7. Allow your puppy to calm down. Puppies soon learn that when they get over-excited, the fun stops. Puppy biting is normal, and we need to have clear boundaries regarding teeth on the skin.

8. Mark the teeth touching the skin with an 'ouch,' but make sure you do not sound angry. That will only excite your dog. Children's voices have a higher pitch, so they are especially exciting to a dog if they say, "ouch." Therefore, I get children to stand still like a tree, lowering everyone's excitement, both dog and child. Then the child must turn away from the dog with their hands crossed against their chest. Again the fun stops, and the dog will start to have good bite inhibition.

9. Once the dog has calmed down, the children can interact with the dog again.

10. With elderly visitors, you cannot afford to have any mouthing whatsoever because their skin is so delicate and punctures easily. I teach an excitable and mouthy puppy to kiss. Often dogs will lick before they start biting. I then use the cue, 'kisses are nice' and immediately give a puppy or adolescent dog a treat. Your dog will soon learn that if s/he licks the back of your hand, you might provide a treat.

11. When your puppy is teething, the puppy biting might get worse, so I always give something other than my hand to chew. Chew toys must be selected carefully. Either use a thermoplastic polymer bone that is indestructible or a chew bone that can be fully and safely digested. Ask your vet for advice.

12. To encourage puppies not to play-bite children, I encourage seeking games for the puppy to play with the child. For example, you can allow your child to encourage their puppy to jump over or crawl under their legs and reward the puppy with a treat. Then you can scatter kibble under a pillow or in an old box for them to find. You can use up to 60% of their food ration for training, so you don't have to worry that they will get fat.

13. Discourage lots of hugging because this can overwhelm a puppy, which may result in a nip from your puppy and, worse still, a bite from an adolescent dog.

Troubleshooting

When puppies are excited with children or elderly grandparents, step in and bring the game to an end. Remember that a tired puppy makes poor decisions, so pop the puppy in its playpen with a calming chew in another room so that that puppy can have a break. Some puppies can become overwhelmed by too much attention. In a typical family home, they need a quiet haven to rest and escape all the hustle and bustle of family life. Puppies need up to seventeen hours of sleep a day.

Teaching Your Dog Recall (Coming Back to You When You Call)

Firstly, I always teach recall as a game with my dogs, even before I put them on a lead. Although I get puppies used to wearing their collar and having a long training line trailing behind them. Loose Leash walking is a prolonged recall, so until a puppy or dog gets used to coming back to you and wanting to stay near you, they are more likely to pull when they are on a lead. Before going outside, I practise the recall game in the living room. Because if a dog does not come back when you ask them to come back in the house, they will not come back when there are many distractions when you are out and about. So, play lots of games where you teach your puppy to pingback to you without outside distractions.

1. First, throw a treat away from you (not far—just into the corner of the room you are training in).

2. As your pup turns to you, say, "*pup pup pup,*" and when they bounce back to you, treat them several times, so they realise what a good deal it is to be close to you.

3. Now you can make the game more challenging— throw the treat into a corner of a room—then run out of the room saying, "*pup pup pup,*" and when they catch up to you, give them a lot of tasty treats (one after the other).

4. To make the game more challenging, hide in different rooms or places (perhaps behind your sofa) and call them using the '*pup pup pup*' cue, and when they find you, don't forget to give them lots of lovely treats.

5. Finally, play the same game in the garden—when you throw the treat away from you, run away as your puppy returns, so the puppy chases you. When your puppy catches up with you, feed your dog lots of treats (one after the other). Or you could give your dog one large piece of something delicious, called a jackpot treat.

6. You are teaching your puppy to gamble when they come to you. You want your dog to think, this time, I might win the Jackpot, which could be some meat leftover from your Sunday Lunch.[44]

7. Now you can also make the game more interesting by using places to hide (perhaps behind your garden shed).

8. Then finally, you can take the game out and about and play hide and seek out on a walk, which taps into your dog's natural desire to hunt. The game now is not just

---

[44] *Take care what you give; no chicken bones as these might perforate a dog's stomach, and some dogs might not tolerate anything rich as it will upset their stomachs. Therefore, be careful about what you offer.*

about food but also taps into the dog's SEEKING system.

Troubleshooting

I like to have a long line on my puppies when I take them out for a walk, where they might get lost if they chase after a squirrel or any other exciting distraction. I always advise puppies to wear a harness and attach a long line on the top ring to prevent a puppy's neck injury if the long line gets caught.

Loose Leash Games

We must first remember that we teach our dogs to pull when we follow them from one new sniff to another. We need our dogs to know that staying close to us is fun. I teach my dogs that being close to me is where all the fun begins. Also, playing games with your dog has bonus consequences in that your dog will start to do exactly the right thing as you go out and about. You don't have to worry about your dog embarrassing you because you have built the relationship first. Play the relationship-boosting games below.

Follow My Hand Game

1. Put your puppy or dog on a long training line and let it trail behind your puppy whilst teaching them to follow your hand.[45]

---

[45] *All my relationship games can start at any age.*

2. First, teach your dog to catch food you drop from your hand—this can take a bit of time with any dog as they have to learn coordination. It is a bit like you patting your head and rubbing your tummy simultaneously. We all find it difficult. So, we have to remember how our dogs find new games difficult. We need to be patient with ourselves as well as our dogs.

3. When your dog knows that food will rain down from your hand, you can walk forward a few steps and watch how your dog magically follows you as he looks up at your hand.

4. Don't forget to praise him by saying "Yes," (or use a clicker, which is a box that makes a click sound every time you press it) every time he steps forward to follow your hand, then drop a piece of food.

Follow Me in Circles

1. Once your dog follows your hand, you can walk in a large circle.

2. Do not wait for your dog. Keep going.

3. You will be surprised that your dog races up to catch up with you.

4. Now practise walking confidently with your dog on both your left and right side.

5. Once they follow your hand you can place your hand on your hip for comfort, but don't forget to drop a treat from your hand now and again.

6. Then practise walking with the dog in a figure of eight.

7. Once you can guarantee your dog will follow, now is the time to pick up the training line.

8. Continue walking in circles and in a figure of eight with you holding the long line at about three feet from your dog's collar (the average length of a lead).

9. You will then find that your pup will continue to watch your hand and will not even notice that you have hold of their leash.

Troubleshooting

Our dogs drag us about only because they have practised that behaviour and been rewarded for it. For example, when we let them haul us to the park, we let them off for a run after pulling. The run in the park then reinforces the pulling on the lead.

Transition Games

These games help with transitioning from environment to environment. Transitions could include walking out of the back door into the garden. It could consist of your dog getting out of the car. Then can your dog calmly wait whilst you get your boots on, ready to go for a walk? We often underestimate how exciting these transitions are.

Practise first transitions between toy to food as a reward (dogs can find transitioning from food to a toy and visa versa punishing). When you swap, realise how much value your dog has for either. You may lose the energy for the game you are using, and you might find your dog will check out their environment. You must get your dog used to transitioning between food and toys and from a high-energy game to a calmer lower-energy game. Think of all the everyday transitions you have to make and the energies between them.

Example of a Transition—Going for a Walk

1. First, practise getting the dog in and out of the car whilst your car is parked in your front drive.

2. Put their leash on.

3. Ask them to sit calmly whilst you open your front door.

4. Walk calmly to your car.

5. Give them the cue to jump into your car (lift your dog if it is still a puppy)

6. Scatter treats in the crate.

7. Give the cue 'free,' and allow them to jump out of the car (or lift them out if still a puppy).

8. Then immediately ask them to pop back into the car.

9. Once your dog has got that and does not get overly excited, then take your dog for a ride in the car.

10. Take your dog to a car park.

11. Carry out the same routine of getting in and out of the crate.

12. Then drive home again.

Troubleshooting

Practising transitioning from one environment to another will help your puppy or dog cope with other transitions he will have to negotiate throughout his life. If you find that they cannot manage at any time, do not proceed to the next stage. Do not be tempted to try and go through all the steps simultaneously. Do not be tempted to take your dog for a walk if they are acting up at any stage. It could take you three weeks to calmly get a dog out of the front door. But if you start with a puppy, you will be ready to go out calmly for the first walk by the time it has had its vaccines. If you have an older rescue dog or a dog with established bad habits, play the game every time you stop for a coffee break. You will be surprised how quickly your dog will catch on that the walk will not happen until they go through each stage calmly.

This Way Game—Switching Direction.

The 'This Way Game' is a great game to play to break the habit of pulling you from sniff to sniff. If your dog starts to pull, remember not to move forward. It is handy to teach your dog how to change direction quickly. Introducing the 'this way' cue helps you quickly get out of difficult situations and improves your dog's focus on you. Also, dogs enjoy quick movement, so they will enjoy the game too.

1. Slide your hand down the lead to the collar. Turn immediately in front of your dog.

2. Now change direction quickly and as your dog follows, feed several treats.

3. Practise several times, and when you can guarantee that your dog knows he is about to change direction when you slide your hand down the lead, add the 'this way' cue.

4. But always say, "this way" before you slide the hand down the lead. Sliding your hand down the lead was an old cue, so you must introduce the new verbal cue before the old cue so that your dog can make the connection. The rule is new cue old cue.

5. Eventually, your dog will shadow your movement with the cue, 'this way,' without having to run your hand down the lead.

6. Play this game out in the garden, then play the game when you are out and about with more distractions.

Troubleshooting

Sometimes our dogs are preoccupied with environmental distractions, from a squirrel to a jogger, a cat, or a bicycle. The list of distractions is endless and can depend on your dog's breed and past experiences. So play the game below, and build your dog's focus on you no matter what the distractions might be.

Chase Me Game

All dogs love to chase. The 'Chase Me Game' is so helpful for any dog. It helps them orient back to you in an emergency. I find this game particularly useful for a dog fond of fence guarding.

1. Throw a treat away from you, and as they go to get the food, say "Yes" as soon as they pick it up.[46]

2. Your dog will turn to you, and when he does, throw the food in the other direction and say "Yes" as he picks up the food.

3. Do this several times.

4. Once your dog has got the idea, next time you can run in the other direction and when he catches up with you, give him plenty of tasty treats.

---

[46] *If playing this game outside the food must be quickly visible to the dog in the grass, otherwise the game becomes a scent game instead of an orientation game.*

5. Now when he realises what fun it is to chase you, a cue can be added; this might be a bop down as if you are going to run, or even a verbal cue, such as, "chase me."

Distraction Game Level Two

The distraction game aims to get your dog used to novelty within the environment. By playing the distraction game, your dog will eventually look to you whenever it is worried or sees something it wants to chase. Distractions can be both good and bad for the dog. What we are trying to achieve is that they will see distractions as none of their business when they are out and about with you.

1. First, put your dog on a lead. Play distraction game level one.

2. As you get to know your dog, you will know what triggers them to bark. Therefore, practise the game far enough away from those triggers at first.

3. When your dog sees a distraction, mark it by saying 'gooood' (draw the word out in reassuring tones) and then give them a treat straight away.

4. Try not to panic if you know the trigger might set your dog off in a fit of barking and lunging. Your dog will pick up your panic on the other end of the lead.

5. As your dog gets better at the game, you will then be able to get closer to his triggers.

6. Do not forget that dogs seek new information, so remember to be vigilant. Watch out for those times your dog takes notice of something new.

7. Eventually, your dog's need to notice or react to distractions will diminish over time.

8. Always give your dog time off in a safe place to go off and sniff and roll and play. Your dog must be given that freedom when not on a lead. I have a cue for my dogs: 'go and be a dog' when I want to give them the freedom to enjoy just being a dog.

Pop Up Game—Going to Bed

Clients love to tell me about their dogs stealing food off the kitchen counter or how they chew just about everything and anything.

As a word of warning, some prevalent items in the house can be highly poisonous to a dog. Houseplants and Chocolate consumption poisoning were the main things we had to treat when we owned our veterinary practice in Cambridge.

Dogs are real opportunists, and if they can find something to steal to eat or chew, they will. So, if you cannot watch your puppy, putting them in a puppy pen is a good idea. I also like to play games to teach my dog to settle on their bed when I prepare food in the kitchen.

Pop Up Game

1. Find a slightly raised dog bed or one with sides.

2. A raised bed or a bed with sides makes it easier for your dog to understand the boundary you are setting.

3. Treat your puppy every time they show interest in the bed.

4. It might be just one paw or two.

5. Say "Yes" or click the clicker whenever they do anything around the bed.

6. Eventually, your puppy will decide to jump up on the bed.

7. Say "Yes" or click and then give your puppy lots of lovely treats one after the other.

8. Now teach your puppy that they only get off their bed when you permit them.

9. Say "free" and throw a treat away from their bed.

10. Now, wait and see what your puppy does.

11. If you have let your dog think things through for themselves, they usually realise that being on their bed will earn rewards, and they will pop up on the bed of their own accord.

12. Say "Yes" and give them lots of tasty treats or even a nice chew so they can settle down and relax. Chewing is a great stress reliever for a puppy.

Calm Game

1. Play the calm game when your puppy has learned to stay on its bed.

2. Drop a treat in front of your puppy's nose whenever you walk past their bed.

Troubleshooting

Some dogs are calm fakers, so you must always wait until they are relaxed and be really good at sneakily feeding them. We often make our puppies into action prompters (asking us for attention) by only paying attention to them when they are excitedly pawing at us.

Mouse Trap Game—Another Version of the Think About It Game

1. Put a few treats on the edge of your dog's bed and cage them under your hand.

2. When your dog politely backs away, say: "Yes," then take a treat and put it behind them. Placing the treat behind them will encourage your dog not to mug you for the treat.

3. Keep doing this until you can guarantee they will always back away from your hand.

4. When you can guarantee they do, start raising your hand completely away from the treat, but if your puppy tries to steal the goodies, then cage the food treats again with your hand.

5. Eventually, your puppy will learn to wait till you permit them to take a treat politely.

Troubleshooting

Sometimes pups can be persistent and start digging at your hand for the treat. I often wear gloves, so their digging doesn't hurt my hands.

Premack Games—To Increase Dog's Motivation

Premack was a Professor of Psychology at the University of Pennsylvania. He discovered that the less desired behaviour (for your dog) could be reinforced by the opportunity to engage in more desired behaviours. In simple terms, do what I want you to do first, and then you get to do what you want. For this game, you create all sorts of fun for your dog. You just have to be inventive and know your dog really well. Does your dog like his walk in the park? Then first, he has to walk on a loose lead before he gets to be let off his leash. But that can be a tough start for your dog. It would be best to show him the rules first with uncomplicated on-the-leash games.

1. Put your dog on its lead.

2. Throw a toy/treat ahead of you, and then restrain.

3. Give them a cue—something they know really well, e.g. sit or down.

4. Then once they have done the behaviour, give them the cue 'get it,' and run with them (making sure that you keep the lead loose).

5. Increase difficulty by restraining the dog first, then throwing the treat.

6. Give the cue for a sit or a down.

7. Once they have performed the behaviour, give them the cue 'get it,' and run with them.

8. Add even more difficulty: Restrain your dog.

9. Throw the treat or toy and give the cue to do a sit or a down at the same time.

10. Once they have performed a sit or a down, give the cue 'get it,' and run with them.

Troubleshooting

When your dog doesn't do the behaviour, don't repeat the cue for sit or down—instead, go and get the treat or toy and give them another chance at playing the game correctly. You are training for exciting real-life distractions, so you need to practise the game so that your dog understands that they need to do what you want before they get to do what they want.

ACKNOWLEDGMENTS

A shower of good blessings to my dog training mentors for making this book possible. I particularly want to thank Joanna Hill, who taught me so much about getting my mechanics right, and being patient when my head was not in the right space.

Thanks must also go to Sunil Raheja, who helped me see how to align my motivations with my dreams. Sunil has been kind enough to affirm my thinking—in a team (the dog and human together), the human part of the relationship must find the right mindset. A good attitude leads to success.

I also want to thank my clients who have been willing to take on my wacky ideas and test them out for me to prove that these methods do work. A special thank you to Dr. Nichola Hendey, my first guinea pig, who became a hero and wrote a new story for her dog.

A special thanks to Felicity Fox, who edited the book and made it all it could be.

ABOUT THE AUTHOR

Yvonne Done is not only passionate about dogs, but she is also passionate about how the relationship with a dog can help a person grow. Her journey to be (in her words) "a better person" started the day she brought her eight-week Border Collie, Fred, home.

Married to a vet for over forty years, Yvonne has always had a dog in the house. However, Yvonne hadn't bargained for a dog like Fred. She never had a pup so willing to play and train. But, working drive in a puppy has its drawbacks. Fred didn't have an off switch. He was either asleep or wanting to do something. There was nothing in-between. Yvonne began to wonder if history was going to repeat itself. She remembered the pain of giving up on her first dog and didn't want to do the same with Fred.

During a vet nurse CPD behaviour course, it was even suggested that Yvonne should rehome Fred. For such a dog as Fred deserved a life on a farm with a job to do. A Border Collie, she was told, does not suit city life. Not only did

Yvonne live in the City of Cambridge, but her home was attached to her husband's veterinary surgery. However, she was determined to help Fred cope so that she could keep him. And so, Yvonne began her journey of doggy enlightenment.

Fred is an inspiration for this book in so many ways. Yvonne's first dog, Sam, was very much on her mind when she wrote her book *In Search of Lassie, A Dog Owner's Guide to the Lassie Myth.* But this book is dedicated to Fred, as it is Fred that helped her become the professional dog trainer and behaviourist she is today.

Yvonne has trained with eminent and respected trainers and has achieved a diploma in animal behaviour with COAPE. But, she continues to study anything and everything about dogs because, in her words; dog training techniques and behavioural studies are continually being revised and revisited. Even in Fred's lifetime, there has been a pendulum swing from complete hands-off training to the idea of dogs being taught how to handle and cope with touch. We as professionals are still finding out what it is to be a dog and how to train them with kind and effective methods.

Even as an English and Drama Teacher, Yvonne has always wanted to be an author, but she didn't expect to be a writer of dog books. Her M.A. was focused on 20th Century Literature. But because of Fred's high work ethic, Yvonne needed to learn about dogs. She found herself reading about everything there was about the modern canine and its welfare. But during her quest, she could not find a book about the broken relationship with a dog and the mental anguish that it causes. And when she looked for trainers to help, no one wanted to know how she felt about her dog's antics. They only wanted to fix her dog, but Yvonne realised she needed fixing too. So during her training and juggling the running of a busy veterinary practice, she employed a business and life coach to help her on her quest. Because of her insights into how she felt when looking for answers for Fred, she mapped out the Game-Plan Vision Worksheets.

Yvonne knows the pain of a challenging dog and not having someone who can understand or help them through that pain. But, Yvonne knows that the gift of curiosity is the key. Through a unique storytelling technique of coaching, Yvonne wants to help everyday owners. Yvonne wants the ordinary owner to understand their own flavour of curiosity so they can push past their comfort zone and learn how to be the better person for their own dog.

Start Your Dog's New Story Here

Lassie Talks

Lassie talks, a dog behaviour and training company was born after publishing my first book, **In Search of Lassie: A Dog Owner's Guide to the Lassie Myth**.

Our company's mission is to help dog owners to understand more about the human and dog relationship and support owners as they build a better bond with their dogs.

This book follows the theme of owning the dog of your dreams, and though you have found that your dog is nothing like Lassie, with game-based training, you can rediscover joy with your dog. With the game-based plans in this book, you will learn how to create the dog you always wanted.

This book has free Projected Story and Game-plan Worksheets, Goal Setting Plans and Daily Planner. Scan the QR code below to download your worksheets, daily planner pages, and three essential dog training skills to help you start your journey today. Plus, an invitation to join Yvonne on your unique and supported programme to become the Hero for your Dog Sidekick and live your dog-owning story.

Please contact us today to learn how we can help you achieve that dream.

Bond with Your Dog

Download Worksheets

Top Training Tips for Dog Owners

Lassie Talks

Why our dogs pull

Training a recall

Tips for a Calm Walk

Rediscover Joy

If you want more help, get in touch with www.lassietalks.com

Milton Keynes UK
Ingram Content Group UK Ltd.
UKHW022016290823
427725UK00017B/155/J